CONTENTS

∾∾∾∾

How to Get Started...

Reading directions is sometimes difficult and hardly ever enjoyable! Most often, people just want to get started. Only if all else fails will they read the instructions. We understand, but please don't approach this study that way. These brief instructions are a vital part of getting started on the right foot and will help you immensely.

FIRST

As you study Jeremiah, you will need four things in addition to this book:

1. A Bible you are willing to mark in. The marking is essential. An ideal Bible for this purpose is *The New Inductive Study Bible (NISB)*. The *NISB* is in a single-column text format with large, easy-to-read type, which is ideal for marking. The margins of the text are wide and blank so you can take notes.

The *NISB* also has instructions for studying each book of the Bible, but it does not contain any commentary on the text, nor is it compiled from any theological stance. Its purpose is to teach you how to discern truth for yourself through the inductive method of study. The charts and maps in the appendix of this study guide are taken from the *NISB*.

Whichever Bible you use, just know you will need to mark in it, which brings us to the second item you will need...

2. A fine-point, four-color ballpoint pen or various colored fine-point pens that you can use to write in your Bible. Office supply stores should have these.

3. Colored pencils or an eight-color leaded Pentel pencil.

4. A composition book or a notebook for working on your assignments and recording your insights.

SECOND

1. As you study Jeremiah, you will be given specific instructions for each day's study. These should take you between 20 and 30 minutes a day, but if you spend more time than this, you will increase your intimacy with the Word of God and the God of the Word.

If you are doing this study in a class and you find the lessons too heavy, simply do what you can. To do a little is better than to do nothing. Don't be an all-or-nothing person when it comes to Bible study.

Remember, anytime you get into the Word of God, you enter into more intensive warfare with the devil (our enemy). Why? Every piece of the Christian's armor is related to the Word of God. And our one and only offensive weapon is the sword of the Spirit, which is the Word of God. The enemy wants you to have a dull sword. Don't cooperate! You don't have to!

2. As you read each passage in the Bible, train yourself to ask the "5 W's and an H": who, what, when, where, why, and how. Asking questions like these helps you see exactly what the Word of God is saying. When you interrogate the text with the 5 W's and an H, you ask questions like these:

What is the chapter about?

Who are the main characters?

When does this event or teaching take place?

Where does this happen?

Why is this being done or said?

How did it happen?

3. Locations are important in many books of the Bible, so marking references to these in a distinguishable way will be helpful to you. We double underline every reference to a location in green (grass and trees are green!) using a four-color ballpoint pen. A few maps are included in the appendix of this book.

4. References to time are also very important and should be marked in an easily recognizable way in your Bible. We mark them by putting a clock like this ⏰ in the margin of the Bible beside the verse where the phrase occurs. You may want to underline or color the references to time in one specific color.

5. You will be given certain key words to mark throughout this study. This is the purpose of the colored pencils and the colored pens. If you will develop the habit of marking your Bible in this way, your study will be significantly more effective and you will retain much more information.

Bible authors repeatedly use *key words* to convey their message to their readers. Certain key words will show up throughout Jeremiah; others will be concentrated in specific chapters. When you mark a key word, you should also mark its synonyms (words that mean the same thing in the context) and any pronouns (*I, me, my, mine; you, your, yours; he, him, his; she, her, hers; it, its; we, us, our, ours; they, them, their, theirs…*) in the same way you marked the key word. Also, mark each word the same way in all of its forms (such as *judge, judgment,* and *judging*).We will give you a few suggestions for ways to mark key words in your daily assignments.

You can use colors or symbols or a combination of colors and symbols to mark words for easy identification. However, colors are easier to distinguish than symbols. When we use symbols, we keep them very simple. For example, you could draw a red heart around the word *love* and shade the inside of the heart like this: love.

When we mark the members of the Godhead (which we do not always mark), we color each word yellow and mark *Father* with a purple triangle like this: **Father.** We mark *Son* this way: **Son** and *Holy Spirit* this way: **Holy Spirit.**

Mark key words in a way that is easy for you to remember.

Devising a color-coding system for marking key words throughout your Bible will help you instantly see where a key word is used. To keep track of your key words, list them on a three-by-five card and mark them the way you mark them in your Bible. You can use this card as a bookmark.

6. A chart called Jeremiah at a Glance is included in the appendix of this book. As you complete your study of a chapter, record the main theme of that chapter under the appropriate chapter number. The main theme of a chapter is what the chapter deals with the most. It may be a particular subject or teaching.

If you will fill out the Jeremiah at a Glance chart in the appendix as you progress through the study, you will have a synopsis of Jeremiah when you are finished. If you have a copy of *The New Inductive Study Bible,* you will find the same chart on pages 1301–1302. If you record your themes there, you will have them for a ready reference.

7. Always begin your study with prayer. As you do your part to handle the Word of God accurately, you must remember that the Bible is a divinely inspired book. The words that you are reading are truth, given to you by God so you can know Him and His ways more intimately. These truths are divinely revealed.

> For to us God revealed them through the Spirit;
> for the Spirit searches all things, even the depths

of God. For who among men knows the thoughts of a man except the spirit of the man which is in him? Even so the thoughts of God no one knows except the Spirit of God (1 Corinthians 2:10-11).

Therefore ask God to reveal His truth to you as He leads and guides you into all truth. He will if you will ask.

8. Each day when you finish your lesson, meditate on what you saw. Ask your heavenly Father how you should live in light of the truths you have just studied. At times, depending on how God has spoken to you through His Word, you might even want to write LFL ("Lessons for Life") in the margin of your Bible and then, as briefly as possible, record the lesson for life that you want to remember.

THIRD

This study is set up so that you have an assignment for every day of the week—so that you are in the Word daily. If you work through your study in this way, you will benefit more than if you do a week's study in one sitting. Pacing yourself this way allows time for thinking through what you learn on a daily basis!

The seventh day of each week differs from the other six days. The seventh day is designed to aid group discussion; however, it's also profitable if you are studying this book individually.

The "seventh" day is whatever day in the week you choose to finish your week's study. On this day, you will find a verse or two for you to memorize and STORE IN YOUR HEART. Then there is a passage to READ AND DISCUSS. This will help you focus on a major truth or major truths covered in your study that week.

We have included QUESTIONS FOR DISCUSSION OR INDIVIDUAL STUDY to assist those using this book in a Sunday school class or a group Bible study. Taking the time to answer these questions will help you apply the truth to your own life even if you are not doing this study with anyone else.

If you are in a group, be sure every member of the class, including the teacher, supports his or her answers and insights from the Bible text itself. Then you will be handling the Word of God accurately. As you learn to see what the text says and compare Scripture with Scripture, the Bible explains itself.

Always examine your insights by carefully observing the text to see what it *says.* Then, before you decide what the passage of Scripture *means,* make sure that you interpret it in the light of its context. Scripture will never contradict Scripture. If it ever seems to contradict the rest of the Word of God, you can be certain that something is being taken out of context. If you come to a passage that is difficult to understand, reserve your interpretations for a time when you can study the passage in greater depth.

The purpose of the Thought for the Week is to share with you what we consider to be an important element in your week of study. We have included it for your evaluation and, we hope, for your edification. This section will help you see how to walk in light of what you learned.

Books in the New Inductive Study Series are survey courses. If you want to do a more in-depth study of a particular book of the Bible, we suggest you do a Precept Upon Precept Bible study course on that book. You may obtain more information on these courses by contacting Precept Ministries International at 800-763-8280 or visiting our website at www.precept.org.

JEREMIAH

INTRODUCTION
TO JEREMIAH

In the Old Testament, God sent His messengers, the prophets, to declare His words to His people and to other nations and their kings. The written records of their messages are filled with phrases like "the Word of the Lord came to" or "thus says the Lord" or "declares the Lord." Often their messages pointed out disobedience that required repentance. Other times they proclaimed judgment for that disobedience, and sometimes they brought comfort. When the message called for repentance, the people sometimes listened to the message, but often they didn't. Listening to God in difficult times can itself be difficult. Bad news is hard to receive. Reactions range from denial ("It can't be true!") to accusation ("You're lying!" or "It's their fault!") to despair ("What will we do?") and even to shooting the messenger, so to speak.

Jeremiah heard it all.

Some of the messages of some of the prophets are recorded in books of the Bible, such as the book of Jeremiah. The Old Testament includes four major prophets (Isaiah, Jeremiah, Ezekiel, and Daniel) and twelve minor prophets. The prophets can also be grouped this way: Those who prophesied before the southern kingdom's captivity in Babylon, like Isaiah, are called *preexilic.* Those who prophesied during the captivity, like Daniel, are called *exilic.* Those who prophesied after the return from the exile, like Malachi, are called *postexilic.* You'll soon discover for yourself when Jeremiah gave his message and whether he should be called preexilic, exilic, or postexilic.

As you study Jeremiah, you'll see the names of kings who reigned during the time he delivered his message, and you'll see references to various events. These clues can help you determine when Jeremiah prophesied. In the appendix of this book, we've included a chart with names and dates to help you put these kings and events in context. But you'll observe the book of Jeremiah to discover Jeremiah's message. You'll also see his emotional turmoil because unlike most prophets, he recorded how he felt while delivering his message. In fact, of all the prophets, Jeremiah is the most personally revealing.

Before you begin studying Jeremiah, let's review a little historical background about the nation of Israel. After God brought Israel out of their 400-year captivity in Egypt and into the land He promised forever to Abraham, Isaac, and Jacob, the people spent about 400 years living without an earthly king because God was their king. Then they asked for a king like the other nations, and God told the prophet Samuel to anoint Saul as king. But Saul was disobedient, so God replaced him with David, with whom He made a covenant to build a dynasty. David's son Solomon succeeded him on the throne and built a temple for God in Jerusalem. But for all the wisdom God gave him, Solomon disobeyed God by turning to the idols his many wives and concubines worshipped. For this sin, in the days of Solomon's son Rehoboam, the kingdom was divided into the northern kingdom (Israel) and the southern kingdom (Judah).

Jeroboam, the first king of the northern kingdom (Israel) immediately created a false, idolatrous worship system, and all the kings of Israel followed in this idolatry, along with almost all the people. (A few went to Judah to worship in Jerusalem at the temple Solomon built, according to God's command.)

Judah fell into idolatry as well even though they had the temple and the Levitical priesthood. God sent messengers, the prophets, to both Israel and Judah but with little result. A few of the kings of Judah responded in obedience. Most did not. Usually, neither the kings nor the people listened to God. By the time Jeremiah began his prophetic ministry, the northern kingdom (Israel) had been taken captive by the Assyrians, they were scattered in a variety of cities and lands, and the territory they had lived in was filled with people from other nations that Assyria brought there. Their descendants included the Samaritans of Jesus' day. God took Israel out of the land He promised them in judgment for their idolatry. Judah watched, but would they learn? Almost 100 years later, God sent Jeremiah with a message. Would the people listen to God this time?

I Knew You
Before I Formed You

～～～～

The start of the book of Jeremiah tells us much about the prophet. We learn about his hometown, his father, and his heritage. We also learn about his relationship with God, which guided his ministry. That's the way it works with us too. Our relationship with God is the most important element of our ministry, or our role in the body of Christ. As you study Jeremiah's message, study the man. Learn from him because God might call you to a ministry like Jeremiah's in your day, declaring the Word of God and calling people to repentance because your nation has sunk into great idolatry. Maybe He already has called you and you need Jeremiah's example to encourage you.

Days One & Two

The book of Jeremiah contains more than his prophecies. It also contains some historical narrative, which provides some context to his message. Historical narrative is best understood by making note of people, places, and events, and people are usually the easiest to see, so let's start there. To get to know key people, mark the references to them in some way.

In order to be consistent in your marking, create a bookmark on something like a three-by-five card. Record your key words on it using the same color and/or symbol you use in your Bible. Then use this as a bookmark for the rest of your study of Jeremiah. Using a bookmark in this way as you go from chapter to chapter will help you mark consistently and save time.

As a general practice, noting geographical references (things you can find on a map) is helpful. We recommend double underlining them in green. Time references, such as the year of a king's reign, are also important in historical narrative. The chapters of Jeremiah are not arranged chronologically, so marking time references is very helpful. As we recommended in "How to Get Started," one technique for marking time references is to draw a clock over them or in the margin of your Bible. Another technique is to simply highlight the phrase in a particular color that you always use for time references.

So here's your first assignment: In your Bible, using the colored pens or pencils we mentioned in "How to Get Started," read Jeremiah 1 and mark every reference to *Jeremiah* in a distinctive way. Later, you can use a different color or symbol or combination for other characters.

Now in a notebook, list what you learn about Jeremiah, including his background, when he ministered, and his reactions.

God is really the central character in the Bible, so we're always interested in His message and activity. Sometimes marking every reference to God in a passage is helpful, but sometimes it's overkill and the page gets too cluttered. You'll have to find your comfort zone with this, but for now, read chapter 1 again and mark the references to God. Then list the key points of God's message to Jeremiah in your notebook.

As you read, mark, and make lists, always ask questions of the text, and let the text provide the answers. Pretend you are an interviewer or investigator, and see if you can identify the who, what, when, where, why, and how of a passage. Make lists with the information you gather by asking these questions.

Looking at chapters paragraph by paragraph is also helpful. Go through chapter 1 again and jot down what each paragraph tells you. For example, what do you learn in verses 1-3? What do you learn in verses 4-10, 11-12, and 13-19? By now you might have also noted a repeated phrase that started the paragraphs. You might choose to mark this phrase throughout Jeremiah as a way of seeing the content clearly.

A little historical background helps in understanding Jeremiah, but in a survey like the New Inductive Study Series, we can't do extensive study. So note the kings mentioned in verses 1-3, look at THE RULERS AND PROPHETS OF JEREMIAH'S TIME in the appendix, and note who reigned when Jeremiah ministered. As we go through the book, you'll find more clues that will help you with the chronology.

Now let's linger on verse 5 a bit and see how it relates to us. Scripture is the best commentary on Scripture, so checking appropriate cross-references will help us understand the truth and apply it to our lives. Read Ephesians 1:3-5; 2:10 and John 15:16. What do you learn?

When you've got the main ideas of the parts of a chapter figured out, determine the main idea or theme of the chapter and record it on JEREMIAH AT A GLANCE in the appendix. When you have completed that chart by listing the themes for all 52 chapters, you'll have your own "table of contents" for future reference. When you want to find a particular topic or event in Jeremiah, you can refer to this chart.

DAY THREE

Every time you open the Word of God, remember that spiritual truth is spiritually discerned. Apart from our resident teacher, the Holy Spirit, we can't comprehend the message of

God. Yes, we can observe words and record content, but the Bible is more than letters on a page. It's God's personal communication to us. Rather than just filling our heads with facts about Jeremiah, we should long to hear God speak to us personally. So don't forget to begin your study time with prayer. Ask God to help you see truth, understand it, and apply it in your life.

Today, read Jeremiah 2 and underline or mark the phrase *the word of the LORD* and similar phrases that indicate that the Lord has delivered a message. This is something you should do throughout Jeremiah, so add it to your bookmark. Idolatry is a major subject too, so mark references to *idols* and add *idolatry* or *idol* to your bookmark. Don't forget to double underline in green any geographical references.

List in your notebook what you learn about idolatry in chapter 2. Then determine a theme for Jeremiah 2 and record it on JEREMIAH AT A GLANCE.

DAY FOUR

Today we'll look at chapter 3, but remember to start in prayer. Now read the chapter and mark the key words on your bookmark. Remember to ask the 5 W's and an H as you go, interrogating the text and thinking about the significance of what you're observing. You probably noticed *adultery* and *harlotry.*[1] Mark them the same way and add them to your bookmark. Did you notice *return?* Did you decide to mark it? Is it important? Noticing key repeated words on your own is an important skill to learn. Mark *return* and add it to your bookmark.

Now list what you learn by marking *adultery* and *harlotry,* and list what they have to do with God's call to return to Him.

Finally, determine a theme for the chapter and add it to JEREMIAH AT A GLANCE.

DAY FIVE

Today, read Jeremiah 4 and mark the key words on your bookmark. Mark *wickedness*[2] and *evil* in the same way and add them to your bookmark.

List what you learn about wickedness and returning to God. Who is evil? Who can return? How? What happens if they don't?

Finally, record the theme of Jeremiah 4 on JEREMIAH AT A GLANCE.

DAY SIX

Now let's summarize the four chapters we've looked at by answering a few questions:

1. What will happen to Judah and why? In what ways do the words *faithless* and *treacherous* describe Judah?

2. How has God held out His hand to call Judah back to Himself? What action do the people need to take? Read Deuteronomy 10:16; 30:6 and Romans 2:29. What relationship do you see?

3. If the people of Judah return, what will happen to them? If they don't return, what will happen to them?

4. What was Jeremiah's role? Read Matthew 28:16-20

and 2 Timothy 4:1-4. How is Jeremiah's mission similar to ours?

DAY SEVEN

 Store in your heart: Jeremiah 1:18-19
Read and discuss: Jeremiah 1:4-10,13-19; 2:1-13,20-28; 3:6-18; 4:1-4,14-18,30-31

QUESTIONS FOR DISCUSSION OR INDIVIDUAL STUDY

∞ Discuss the setting of Jeremiah 1. Who reigns, and what do you know about the history of Judah?

∞ Discuss Jeremiah's call and God's message to him regarding the opposition he'll face. What application can you make? What message of judgment for idolatry has God given Christians?

∞ How will God judge Judah? Why will they be judged this way?

∞ What do you learn about the nation that God will use to judge Judah?

∞ What hope does God hold out for Judah? What does this tell you about God?

THOUGHT FOR THE WEEK

What does God do with rebellious people? Does He have unlimited patience? Does He judge righteously? God called Jeremiah to deliver a message to Judah that they would be judged for their idolatry. God said He would send a nation from the north to bring judgment on Judah. At the same time, Jeremiah was to prophesy to the nations that God was ruler of all.

God knew Jeremiah, just as He knows you and me. God knew that the people wouldn't listen to His message of judgment, but would resist it because they didn't want to believe that life would soon be very difficult for them. He also knew that the kings, princes, priests, and people of Judah could be intimidating to Jeremiah, so He gave Jeremiah a message that strengthened him.

Does God operate that way with Christians? Does He call us to do difficult things for Him? Does He know how intimidating people can be? And does He give us a message that strengthens us in our task? The answer to all these questions is yes.

The Gospels and Acts show us that some people will resist the message of the Savior. The examples of Peter, James, John, and Paul are enough to show that such resistance can be physically dangerous. Most of us in the West don't face physical violence because of our faith or our efforts to spread the good news, but people do in other parts of the world, and that physical violence sometimes ends in death. In the West, we rarely face anything worse than ridicule, rejection, and strained relationships. Sometimes people lose their jobs, but almost no one is arrested for their faith or for sharing the gospel.

Still, our work isn't always easy. How does God sustain us in this difficult task? What message has He given us in His Word that helps us in our faith? Does He make us "as a fortified city and as a pillar of iron and as walls of bronze," as He promised He would do for Jeremiah (Jeremiah 1:18)? And if He does, what do those metaphors mean in our everyday lives?

God told Jeremiah that even though the kings, princes, priests, and people would fight against him, they would not overcome him. God would deliver Jeremiah from them.

We have an adversary—Satan. He is the source behind the opposition in the world against God and against God's people. And God's promise to His people is that they will not be overcome, but will be overcomers. The source of our strength is in John 16:33: "These things I have spoken to you, so that in Me you may have peace. In the world you have tribulation, but take courage; I have overcome the world."

Because Jesus has overcome the world, we can have courage and peace even in the tribulation we have in the world. Knowing this, Paul wrote, "Do not be overcome by evil, but overcome evil with good" (Romans 12:21). Similarly, John wrote, "For whatever is born of God overcomes the world; and this is the victory that has overcome the world—our faith. Who is the one who overcomes the world, but he who believes that Jesus is the Son of God?" (1 John 5:4-5).

So there it is. We who have faith are overcomers because we have saving faith in the Lord Jesus Christ. He is our strength and gives us courage. And so John writes to the churches of Asia in the Revelation that they who overcome will not be hurt by the second death, which is reserved for unbelievers. Instead, they will...

- ✿ eat from the tree of life in the paradise of God
- ✿ have authority over the nations
- ✿ receive hidden manna and a white stone with a new name
- ✿ be clothed in white garments
- ✿ be pillars in the temple of God
- ✿ sit down with Jesus on His throne.

Check it out. Read Revelation 2–3. See for yourself. And let those truths encourage you to persevere in delivering God's truth and to listen to God in difficult times.

If There Is One Who Seeks Truth

What will it take for God to relent from His warning of destruction? Will He destroy the righteous with the unrighteous, or will He spare the unrighteous for the sake of the righteous? In Abraham's time, God said He would spare Sodom and Gomorrah if He could find ten righteous persons there. Now, centuries later, He promises to spare Jerusalem if He can find even one.

Day One

Read Jeremiah 5, marking the key words on your bookmark. Add *truth* and *destroy*[3] (including *destruction*[4]) to your bookmark and mark them also. When you're done, read the chapter again, looking for the nation who is coming from afar. You can mark every reference, but you don't need to add it to your bookmark. Remember to ask the 5 W's and an H as you go. Read with a purpose and not simply to color!

Now list in your notebook what you learn about that nation and the destruction it will cause. Also list what you learn about the wicked. Everything you list will answer one of the 5 W's and an H.

Compare Jeremiah 5:14-19 with Deuteronomy 28:49-55.

Finally today, determine the theme of Jeremiah 5 and record it on JEREMIAH AT A GLANCE in the appendix.

DAY TWO

Read Jeremiah 6 today and mark the key words on your bookmark. Mark *hear* and *listen*[5] the same way and add them to your bookmark. There is so much more that could be marked if you were studying in greater depth. We've chosen these few words as the most important.

What's the main subject of this chapter? Write this out as a theme for Jeremiah 6 and record it on JEREMIAH AT A GLANCE.

DAY THREE

Read Jeremiah 7 and mark the key words on your bookmark. Mark *temple* (*house*) in a special way. List in your notebook what you learn from marking *temple*. Who prophesied there, and what was the message? Why was this message given? What provoked God? What were the people saying about the temple? What did that mean?

DAYS FOUR & FIVE

It's time for a little historical background so you can appreciate what's going on in these chapters. The temple was the center of worship in Judah. Read 2 Chronicles 6, part of the record of the temple's dedication by Solomon. In Jeremiah,

Judah stands on the brink of captivity. Have the people forgotten 2 Chronicles 6:36-39? Why do you answer this way?

Before Solomon built the temple in Jerusalem, God's people met Him at the portable tabernacle that had been built at Mount Sinai. When they entered the promised land, the tabernacle rested at Shiloh for nearly 400 years. But what happened according to Jeremiah 7:12? Read 1 Samuel 4:1-10,22 for the beginning of the end for Shiloh. Then read Psalm 78:54-64 about the tabernacle at Shiloh. How does this relate to Jeremiah 7?

Later, some kings defiled Solomon's temple. Read 2 Kings 16:1-4; 21:1-9.

But has it been this way continually? Are there no bright spots? Read 2 Kings 23:4-12.

Read Matthew 21:12-13 and relate this to Jeremiah's day.

What have you learned in these two days of study about worship and obedience from the heart? What can you apply to your life?

Finally, determine the theme of Jeremiah 7 and record it on JEREMIAH AT A GLANCE.

DAY SIX

Read Jeremiah 8 and mark the key words on your bookmark. Add *deceit* to your bookmark. Remember to mark synonyms like *lying*.[6]

The start of chapter 8 includes an important time phrase. How does that link chapter 8 with chapter 7?

How does Jeremiah feel about what he knows? Have you seen this in earlier chapters?

Now read through the chapter again and in the margin of your Bible, note what the people trusted in.

Record the theme of Jeremiah 8 on JEREMIAH AT A GLANCE.

DAY SEVEN

 Store in your heart: Jeremiah 6:14

Read and discuss: Jeremiah 5:1-9,21-29; 6:22-26; 7:1-20,30-34; 8:8-22

QUESTIONS FOR DISCUSSION OR INDIVIDUAL STUDY

- From what you read in the cross-references, how did the Israelites treat the tabernacle and the temple? What were they doing in the days of Jeremiah? Is this right or wrong?

- What parallels to modern times can you find in the way the people of Judah and Jerusalem treated the temple?

- How did all this prophecy affect Jeremiah? How does he react to the message from the Lord?

- What did you learn about the nations coming from afar to judge Israel? How does this compare to what you saw last week?

- Discuss the justice of God's judgment. Has He given the people fair warning? Should He judge them? Make sure to support your answers with Scripture.

- What application to your life can you draw from this week's lesson?

THOUGHT FOR THE WEEK

First the tabernacle and then the temple were the places God chose to meet with His covenant people, Israel. The people came with sacrifices to worship God according to the Law, the covenant He made with them at Mount Sinai. But as God clearly told Saul, obedience is better than sacrifice. Anyone can bring a sacrifice in strict obedience to the letter of the law. But what about obedience from the heart?

We can fall into the same trap today. We can attend church with strict obedience without worshipping from the heart. If we truly embrace the experience of worship and the value of a weekly public worship service, we should be glad for opportunities to worship God. If we long to spend time with God because we love Him with all our heart, all our soul, all our mind, and all our strength, we should also rejoice in our times when we talk to Him in prayer and hear from Him in our Bible study. Or we can do these things simply to obey the letter of the law, checking off our to-do list rather than taking pleasure in our relationship with God.

Can you imagine having a human relationship based on adherence to rules and expectations? I call my wife because that's what husbands are supposed to do—check. But if my heart is not in it, then my actions are deceptive. We visit our families because we are obliged to—check. But if we are acting merely out of obligation, we are not experiencing true relationship. We bring a tithe or offering to church because we're expected to—check. But if we give grudgingly, we are not expressing our love and trust to God.

How easy it is to give lip service to worship but remain far from the true experience of it. We can rationalize our actions, saying, "I'm not bowing down to an idol and burning incense to it. I'm not that bad." But we might as well be because if our heart is far from worshipping God, in effect we're worshipping something or someone else. The church may be where we go to attend, but if we're just going through the motions, we're deceiving ourselves and others. But God cannot be deceived.

Just as in Jeremiah's days, God recognizes true worship.

He's never fooled. He knows you, He knows your heart, and He knows the difference between genuine worship and show.

So what's the tie between Jeremiah's experience and our own day? God's Word. Jeremiah brought God's message to the people of Israel, calling them to repent of their ways and return to Him. The book of Jeremiah brings us God's message today, calling us to repent of our own ways and to return to Him. Israel was generally disobedient and idolatrous for hundreds of years, and God was patient. He'll be patient with us, but we don't have hundreds of years. We have this life. But God holds out that same invitation for us to return to Him if we've strayed from pure devotion to Him.

And God's messengers, our pastors and Bible teachers who deliver God's Word, feel a lot like Jeremiah when they see sheep straying. They hurt when they see anything but true worship of God. They're not perfect, of course, but they know, they care, and it hurts. They may have gone through a similar time and may know exactly what we're going through, and it hurts them to see us go through it too. But changing our ways because they hurt is not the answer. Changing our ways because of our relationship with God is the only right motivation. That matters only if we love God, because we never want to hurt those we truly love.

So examine yourself today. Maybe it's time to hear God's message and listen, to pay attention to the trumpet of the watchmen. Maybe you know some people who need this message. If you love them, share it with them so they don't miss out on the loving relationship you have with God. If only they'll listen to God.

THE LIVING GOD

Do you really believe the Lord is the true God? The living God? The everlasting King? If so, are you living accordingly? Is your life submitted to the reality of living with Him for all eternity, or do you live for the here and now, the moment?

DAYS ONE & TWO

We're so glad you want to know your God and His Word better. Begin this week in prayer, knowing you're not alone. Begin each day of study in prayer, because spiritual things are spiritually appraised. Ask God to lead you to truth.

As usual, we'll begin by reading with a purpose, marking key words and interrogating the text with the 5 W's and an H. Read Jeremiah 9 and mark the key words from your bookmark. Also mark references to *weeping* or *tears,* but don't add those words to your bookmark. Jeremiah is often called the weeping prophet. These references occur occasionally throughout Jeremiah. You may note them, but you don't have to mark them all the time.

Do you remember that in Jeremiah 1 we learned that he was appointed a prophet to the nations, not just Judah? Who does God prophesy judgment against in Jeremiah 9? What are the implications of this? Does God judge every nation that does not acknowledge Him?

In our day, Jews read Jeremiah 8:22–9:22 every year in their synagogues in memory of and mourning for the destruction of the temple by the Babylonians in 586 BC and by the Romans in AD 70. The Jews who returned from Babylon started rebuilding the first temple only 70 years after the Babylonians destroyed it. But more than 1900 years have passed since the Roman destruction of the second temple, with no rebuilding—truly a cause for mourning.

Compare Jeremiah 9:7 with 6:27. What is God going to do through Jeremiah? Does this relate to us in any way? Compare 9:9 with 5:9,29. You might want to write these cross-references in the margin of your Bible. Besides the people of Judah, what is affected? Look at verse 12.

Look at 9:16. Will everyone be annihilated? Comparing Scripture with Scripture helps us understand properly. We know that Scripture never contradicts Scripture, so compare this verse with Jeremiah 4:27; 5:18.

Finally, determine a theme for Jeremiah 9 and record it on JEREMIAH AT A GLANCE in the appendix.

DAY THREE

Today we're going to look at Jeremiah 10. As you mark the key words from your bookmark, you'll be able to see the main point easily. But pay close attention because careful observation is the key to accurate interpretation and valid application.

Now make a list of what you learn about the idols and those who make them. Be sure to note the consequences of being "stupid and foolish" (verse 8) like the men and shepherds of Israel.

In contrast of what you learn about idols, you also can make a pretty nice list of what you learn about God from this chapter. Contrasts like this one are always important to note when you're studying God's Word. Authors contrast things in order to highlight differences. One way to see the contrast well is to make your lists side by side—one column for idols, and one column for God.

Finally, determine a theme for Jeremiah 10 and record it on JEREMIAH AT A GLANCE.

Day Four

Today, let's review what we've seen so far in Jeremiah so we don't lose the overall message as we focus on details day by day.

What did you learn in Jeremiah 1? What happened?

What did you learn in Jeremiah 2–6? Summarize the message.

What did you learn in Jeremiah 7–10? Summarize the message.

Read Jeremiah 7:1-7 again (and 11:1-6) and note where God told Jeremiah to deliver his messages.

Day Five

Today we're ready to move on. Read Jeremiah 11 and mark the key words from your bookmark. Mark *covenant* by shading it red and outlining in yellow. This is a key word throughout the Bible, so consistent marking is helpful. Don't forget to add it to your bookmark. Note where Jeremiah is to preach his message. Does his message change?

Which covenant does Jeremiah refer to? What do you learn about it? How does it relate to idols? Read Exodus 20:1-6. How does the covenant relate to the coming judgment? Read Deuteronomy 11:8-17,26-32.

Now determine a theme for Jeremiah 11 and record it on JEREMIAH AT A GLANCE.

DAY SIX

Read Jeremiah 12 and mark the key words from your bookmark. Pay attention to who is speaking to whom. Also mark *My inheritance*,[7] but don't add it to your bookmark.

If you don't understand what God's inheritance is, look up Jeremiah 2:7; 3:18-19; and 10:16.

You might have noticed *uproot*[8] and *built*[9] and remembered that these ideas were mentioned in Jeremiah 1. If not, review Jeremiah's commission in Jeremiah 1:10.

Determine a theme for Jeremiah 12 and then record it on JEREMIAH AT A GLANCE.

DAY SEVEN

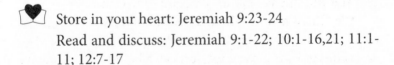 Store in your heart: Jeremiah 9:23-24
Read and discuss: Jeremiah 9:1-22; 10:1-16,21; 11:1-11; 12:7-17

QUESTIONS FOR DISCUSSION OR INDIVIDUAL STUDY

 ∽ Discuss what you observed about deceit and its consequences.

∾ Who is the wise man? Where does understanding come from? What is your role in becoming wise?

∾ Contrast idols and God. How might things in your life compare to these idols?

∾ How does your life reflect your knowledge of God?

∾ Discuss how God's actions and words in Jeremiah relate to His covenant with Israel.

∾ Discuss the importance of keeping promises.

∾ Discuss the consequences for disobedience and the promise that is ours if we learn God's ways.

∾ Leave time for discussion of specific things in your group's lives—personal application, not just theoretical Bible knowledge.

Thought for the Week

Idolatry is a recurring theme in the Old Testament. Israel had a special place among all the nations of the earth. God chose them to be His people so they would be a light to the nations, showing all the people of the earth what God is like and demonstrating the blessings of being His people. To help Israel do this, God spoke through the prophets and compared Himself with the false gods of the other nations.

We Christians also hold a special place with respect to God. The apostle Peter's encouragement applies to us: "You are a chosen race, a royal priesthood, a holy nation, a people for God's own possession, so that you may proclaim the excellencies of Him who has called you out of darkness into His marvelous light" (1 Peter 2:9).

So just as ancient Israel had a specific calling in their own time, we have a similar purpose in our time. Israel was one people descended from Abraham, Isaac, and Jacob, with one language, one set of customs, one heritage. We, the church, come from a multitude of peoples, we speak many languages, and we have varied heritages. But we have one purpose—to proclaim the excellencies of God, who called us.

So what are these excellencies? Jeremiah 10 highlights some in contrast to the idols that Israel foolishly worshipped.

> The Lord is the true God;
> He is the living God and the everlasting King…
> It is He who made the earth by His power,
> Who established the world by His wisdom;
> And by His understanding He has stretched
>   out the heavens.
> When He utters His voice, there is a tumult of
>   waters in the heavens,
> And He causes the clouds to ascend from the
>   end of the earth;
> He makes lightning for the rain,
> And brings out the wind from His storehouses
>   (Jeremiah 10:10,12-13).

And yet some people would rather worship "the work of the hands of a craftsman" (Jeremiah 10:3). Oh, don't laugh. Things hadn't gotten much better by the time the New Testament was written in the midst of pagan Roman culture. Pagan idols and their temples were all around, and the comparison was easy to see. Idolatry is still big business, but today, the idols masquerade as other things.

Look around and see what people worship today—what takes first place in their lives: money, business, hobbies, sports, leisure. All these take first place for different people. Just measure the time spent on them compared to time spent with the Lord in prayer, in Bible study, in worship, and in the good works He calls us to do.

Our call is to live today in the light of eternity with God. Yes, we can enjoy life and the things we have, but they have no eternal significance, and when we go to be with the Lord, we won't be taking them with us. All we take with us into eternity is our relationship with the eternal God and the record of our lives—how we served Him, how we lived for Him, how we worshipped Him by what we did. For those things alone we receive eternal reward.

DOES SORROW LEAD TO REPENTANCE?

∽∾∽∾∽

There are two kinds of sorrow. One—the sorrow that recognizes the wrong toward someone else, such as God—leads to repentance. It's based on your love for others. The other—the sorrow that comes simply because you got caught and punished—doesn't lead to repentance because it's self-oriented. It's about what happened to you.

DAY ONE

Read Jeremiah 13 today and mark the key words from your bookmark. Notice the comparisons God uses to communicate and the way these word pictures illuminate our understanding.

"The king and the queen mother" are mentioned in verse 18. Read 2 Kings 24:8-15. How does this help explain the message of this chapter and help you place it in time? Look at the chart THE RULERS AND PROPHETS OF JEREMIAH'S TIME in the appendix and note where chapter 13 fits. Then read Jeremiah 13:13 again. Is Jehoiachin the only king who will be "filled with drunkenness"?

Now determine the theme for Jeremiah 13 and record it on JEREMIAH AT A GLANCE.

DAY TWO

Read Jeremiah 14 today and mark the key words from your bookmark. Add *sword, famine,* and *pestilence.*[10] Some prefer to mark all three the same way. Others have distinct markings. It's your choice.

What are the first 9 verses about? What is Israel saying? How does God respond in verse 10?

Jeremiah and the Lord have a conversation that begins in verse 11. What is it about? What will the end result be?

What do you learn about the different people groups mentioned in this chapter?

Determine the theme of Jeremiah 14 and record it on JEREMIAH AT A GLANCE.

DAYS THREE & FOUR

Read Jeremiah 15 and mark the key words from your bookmark. Note who is speaking and to whom. You might want to mark these in the margin of your Bible.

Compare verses 19-21 to Jeremiah 1:17-19. Why did God repeat Himself here? Look at Jeremiah 15:10,15-18. As we said earlier, historical background helps in understanding Jeremiah. Reading through 1 and 2 Kings and 2 Chronicles will do the job, but that will take more time than we have right now—perhaps another study or two for you in the New Inductive Study Series. But in Jeremiah 15, Manasseh, son of Hezekiah and king of Judah, is mentioned as the reason God will do what He plans. Read 2 Kings 21:1-18 and 2 Chronicles 33:1-20 to see what Manasseh did.

Manasseh's story is even more important because of his father, Hezekiah. That's a longer story. Read 2 Kings 18–20 and 2 Chronicles 29–32. Judah had only four good kings after David and Solomon—Asa, Jehoshaphat, Hezekiah, and Josiah. The contrast between Hezekiah and his son makes Jeremiah's words even more poignant.

Now determine a theme for chapter 15 and record it on JEREMIAH AT A GLANCE.

DAYS FIVE & SIX

Read Jeremiah 16 and mark the key words from your bookmark. Add *calamity*[11] to your bookmark. Also read Amos 3:6 and mark *calamity* there. But does calamity rule out the possibility of compassion? What is Israel's future according to Jeremiah 16:14-21?

God is personal with Jeremiah throughout the book, but here He tells him not to marry or have children because of the judgment to come. If you'd like to understand Jeremiah even better, make a biographical sketch of the prophet. Simply go through all 16 chapters we've studied so far, and list what you learn about Jeremiah. Look at the way he expresses himself and God's response to him. It's a bit like journaling, but you're making a journal about Jeremiah. He's so human, so vulnerable...so *real*, isn't he?

How would you compare Jeremiah's life to your own? His society and ours?

Now determine a theme for Jeremiah 16 and record it on JEREMIAH AT A GLANCE.

Finally, Beloved, what is God's lesson for us? What can we apply to our lives?

DAY SEVEN

 Store in your heart: Jeremiah 15:16

Read and discuss: Jeremiah 13:1-14; 14:10-22; 15:10-21; 16:1-9,14-21

QUESTIONS FOR DISCUSSION OR INDIVIDUAL STUDY

- ∞ Discuss Jeremiah's character, particularly his feelings for God and for his people. What do you see that you can apply to your life? How do you feel about the sin around you? How do you express this to God?

- ∞ Is God a righteous judge? Discuss God's reasons for judging Judah—their outward behavior and their inner attitude.

- ∞ Is God compassionate? Discuss what you learned about God's compassion.

- ∞ What do you learn about God's methods of calling people to account for their sin? Is this part of judgment? Do these kinds of things (sword, famine, pestilence) happen today? Are they expressions of God's judgment or "Mother Nature"?

THOUGHT FOR THE WEEK

Three times so far in Jeremiah (chapters 5; 8; and 15), God has declared that Israel has not repented. What is repentance? The Hebrew word translated *repent* in these three places is transliterated *shuv.* It refers to a turning around, returning, or turning back, especially of turning from evil and turning toward good. Jeremiah 4 also uses other expressions, like "circumcise yourselves to the LORD and remove the foreskins of your heart" and "wash your heart from evil." But these are subsumed in the meaning of *shuv.*

The word is used in Jeremiah more than any other book of the Bible, and along with those many phrases that describe repentance, its frequent use makes repentance a key theme throughout the book of Jeremiah. God asks and expects Israel to repent of their idolatry. And if they do not repent, He will judge them. That was the message that was so hard for Israel and Judah to hear and receive. They didn't understand that the judgment was connected to their failure to listen to God and obey Him.

And when God declares that Judah has not repented, He also says He is tired of relenting, or changing His mind. It's important to understand that God is not a man, nor is He like man, who changes his mind. The way man changes his mind is borne of uncertainty or whim. God relents of judgment, waiting for man's repentance because He is compassionate and long-suffering. God patiently waits and gives yet another chance. He compassionately stays His hand of judgment. The fact that He relents has nothing to do with whim or uncertainty.

God's judgment is just, but it is not divorced from His compassion or long-suffering. He gave mankind 100 years in Noah's day. He's given us almost 2000 years since Jesus paid the price of our sin. Referring to the day of judgment and destruction known as the "day of the Lord," Peter wrote, "The Lord is not slow about His promise, as some count slowness, but is patient toward you, not wishing for any to perish but for all to come to repentance" (2 Peter 3:9).

In fact, Judah's judgment was already long overdue by man's standard of patience. The kingdom of Israel split after Solomon died in 931 BC because of Solomon's adulterous idolatry. The northern kingdom (Israel) immediately went into idolatry and never stopped despite continuous warnings through the prophets. God relented for more than 200 years before sending them into captivity by Assyria.

The southern kingdom (Judah) was not continuously idolatrous as Israel was, and it had an additional 100 years and more of God's forbearance, additional prophets, and the clear example set by God's dealings with Israel. Still, the people of Judah maintained their false trust in the temple. They also trusted in the words of false prophets, who assured the people that judgment wouldn't come. They deceived themselves by listening to such words. And God still relented, giving chance after chance for them to repent.

This is very much like the way God deals with the world today, not wishing for any to perish, but for all to come to repentance. Aren't you glad that God relents? But how long will He? Just like Israel and Judah, we will see a day when relenting ends and judgment comes.

Blessed Is the Man Whose Trust Is the Lord

Cursed is the man who trusts in mankind
And makes flesh his strength,
And whose heart turns away from the LORD...
[But] blessed is the man who trusts in the LORD
And whose trust is the LORD.
For He will be like a tree planted by the water...
And it will not be anxious in a year of drought
Nor cease to yield fruit (Jeremiah 17:5,7-8).

Days One & Two

After prayer, read Jeremiah 17 without marking anything. Read it a second time and mark the key words on your bookmark. Also mark the word *heart*.

Now let's dig in a little deeper. Heart issues are exposed in chapter 17 more than any other place in Jeremiah even though the word *heart* is used most in chapter 4. Did you mark *heart* in chapter 4? If not, take a few moments to do that now and note what you learn. Then list what you learned from marking *heart* in Jeremiah 17.

Mark the word *trust(s)* in Jeremiah 17:5-8 and note what you learn.

What had Judah been trusting in—the Lord or man? The Lord's word or man's? What about you?

Keeping the Sabbath was important for Israel because it was an outward sign to men and a demonstration that the Israelites were God's covenant people. Read these cross-references:

> Genesis 2:1-3
>
> Exodus 20:8-11
>
> Exodus 31:12-17
>
> Numbers 15:32-36
>
> Deuteronomy 5:12-15

How does breaking the Sabbath relate to the rest of the chapter about the heart and trust?

Record a theme for Jeremiah 17 on JEREMIAH AT A GLANCE.

Day Three

Now read Jeremiah 18 and mark key words found on your bookmark and any other key words, including *nation* and *calamity.*

Now let's look more closely at the word of the Lord from the potter's house to Israel. What does God want His people to know about Himself? About people—the nations and Israel?

How will Judah and Jerusalem respond to God's offer in Jeremiah 18:11? What does this tell you about their state of mind? What is their response to Jeremiah as God's spokesman? We'll see more about their response to Jeremiah and his message in later chapters.

What truth from the analogy of the potter can you apply to yourself?

Finally, determine a theme for Jeremiah 18 and record it on JEREMIAH AT A GLANCE.

DAY FOUR

Read Jeremiah 19 to get an overview of the chapter. Now read it again, marking key words from your bookmark and any others you find, including the reference to *the LORD's house* (mark it the same way you have marked *temple*).

The Lord uses another great word picture related to pottery. What is it, and how does He use it to make His point? Note the location. Remember to double underline in green all of the places you can find on a map. Check this one on JERUSALEM IN THE TIME OF JEREMIAH in the appendix.

Read 2 Kings 23:1-10 to see some of the reforms that Josiah, Manasseh's grandson, instituted to purge the land of Manasseh's evils.

Why is the jar shattered? What is going to happen in Jerusalem—why are their ears going to tingle? Who is behind this calamity?

Record the main theme of chapter 19 on JEREMIAH AT A GLANCE.

DAYS FIVE & SIX

Now observe Jeremiah 20. Mark the key words on your bookmark and add *Babylon*. Remember, as you mark, you're reading with a purpose. You should always be asking the 5 W's and an H as you read and mark. Don't get in a hurry and turn this into a coloring contest. Make the most of your precious time in the Word of God.

How do Jeremiah 19 and 20 connect?

Who is Pashhur, and what does he do? What does Jeremiah prophesy about Pashhur after he is released from the stocks?

The upper Benjamin Gate was probably the upper gate of

the temple built by Jotham. However, there was also a Benjamin Gate in the city wall, probably the same gate called the Sheep Gate (see JERUSALEM IN THE TIME OF JEREMIAH in the appendix).

Now let's turn our attention to Jeremiah. What can you add to your biographical sketch of him? Can you relate to Jeremiah in any way? How do you handle *your* thoughts and emotions in difficult circumstances?

Finally, determine a theme for Jeremiah 20 and record it on JEREMIAH AT A GLANCE.

DAY SEVEN

 Store in your heart: Jeremiah 17:7-8

Read and discuss: Jeremiah 17; 18:1-18; 19; 20

QUESTIONS FOR DISCUSSION OR INDIVIDUAL STUDY

- ∞ Discuss your insights about Jeremiah. What does he say about himself? Why does he say these things?

- ∞ Can you identify with Jeremiah? Have you ever felt as he does? Discuss specific issues that cause you to feel this way.

- ∞ Discuss the visual aids God tells Jeremiah to use. How do they help you understand God, His ways, and His message?

- ∞ What are some of the specific things Israel did to incur God's wrath? What do they need to do about them to avoid His wrath?

◈ What do you learn about God's mercy? How does this affect your life?

Thought for the Week

God is a loving God. He is love, and He loves you. But what does love look like? How does love act? Does love seek what's best for the other? What if stern warning and judgment are what's best? Is love tough enough for that?

What does love look like when God is the Father and Israel and Judah are the children, or God is the husband and Israel is God's wife? What does the God of love do when His wife commits adultery?

Was God expressing His love when He sent the northern kingdom (Israel) into captivity to teach the southern kingdom (Judah) a lesson? Was He loving when He threatened Judah with captivity? Did He demonstrate his love when He killed some of the people of Judah with the sword, famine, and pestilence, or when He brought such severe conditions on them that they resorted to cannibalism? Is that love?

Maybe those actions are expressions of tough love, or maybe they show God's standards of justice. Either way, you can't deny that Judah had plenty of warning and many chances. You can't deny God's patience. After all, this idolatry had been going on for hundreds of years, and except for a few godly kings who followed the Lord and Josiah's cleansing of the temple and the land, idolatry was pretty much the norm in Judah.

So what do you do when you make covenants with people and love them? Do you let them go their way, or do you try whatever it takes to bring them back? How strong is your love? God takes drastic measures with Judah. He will use the Babylonians to demonstrate to Judah that He is in charge and can do as He pleases. The people of Judah were trusting in the temple and God's promise to them about that place. They thought He would never abandon His temple or Jerusalem or them regardless of how they acted. They were wrong.

God warned Judah through a succession of prophets. He showed them He meant business by having Assyria take Israel captive. But still Judah persisted in the belief that they were too special for that kind of treatment because they had the temple and Jerusalem, and God would never abandon those. Or so they thought.

And because of this trust in the temple, they did not repent of their idolatry. So in His tough love God warned them that they would suffer under the sword, famine, pestilence, and captivity if they did not repent. That was the promise.

God appointed Jeremiah to bring this hard message, and as you might expect, he and his message were rejected and opposed. Being God's spokesman wasn't an easy task when the message was so harsh. But God had also promised Jeremiah that the people wouldn't overcome him.

So it is with us. We are called to proclaim a message of salvation, and people often reject and oppose it. These people aren't open to the idea that there is a God who judges all men and that there is only one way to avoid punishment. This is seen as narrow-minded or exclusivist. Modern culture shouts for us to be tolerant, open-minded, and nonjudgmental. When we proclaim the gospel, people reject us along with our message. But they are actually rejecting God, not us. If we take their response personally, we can become weary of doing good, fainthearted, and discouraged. God knew this could happen to Jeremiah, so He gave him this promise:

> "Now behold, I have made you today as a fortified
> city and as a pillar of iron and as walls of bronze
> against the whole land, to the kings of Judah, to
> its princes, to its priests and to the people of the

> land. They will fight against you, but they will not overcome you, for I am with you to deliver you," declares the LORD (Jeremiah 1:18-19).

God has promised us too.

> For whatever is born of God overcomes the world; and this is the victory that has overcome the world—our faith. Who is the one who overcomes the world, but he who believes that Jesus is the Son of God? (1 John 5:4-5).

We need not fear rejection and opposition. God has made us overcomers. So *we* need to listen to God in difficult times, fight the good fight, finish the course, and keep the faith.

WHOSE WORD
IS TRUTH?

Voices with conflicting messages speak to us from many directions today, even from within the church. Whose voice speaks truth? How do you know whom to believe? Is everyone who says he speaks for the Lord trustworthy? The people of Judah also had many voices speaking to them. What did they do?

DAY ONE

So far, the text of Jeremiah hasn't included many time references that we can use to understand when the chapters occur. The focus has been on the message without regard to who was king or to Babylon's attacks against Judah and Jerusalem. But starting with Jeremiah 21, the text begins to give clues of when the messages are delivered. The chapters don't appear in chronological sequence, but we need to pay attention to the kings.

So today, read Jeremiah 21, mark the key words, and note which king is ruling Judah. Also read Jeremiah 20:1. Are these the same Pashhur? Read 2 Kings 25:1-2 and then look at THE RULERS AND PROPHETS OF JEREMIAH'S TIME in the appendix to see when this chapter occurs.

Summarize the message of the chapter into a theme and record it on JEREMIAH AT A GLANCE.

DAYS TWO & THREE

After beginning in prayer, read Jeremiah 22 and mark any key words you find. Several kings are mentioned, so note each, referring to THE RULERS AND PROPHETS OF JEREMIAH'S TIME. Summarize the prophecy about each king. Now read 2 Chronicles 36:1-10. When were these prophecies given? Did they come to pass? Who ruled after Jeconiah? Was this man a son of Jeconiah?

A little historical background (which you can find in commentaries) is helpful if you haven't studied Kings and Chronicles. Jeremiah includes several historical chapters, as we'll see later, but the bare outline of events will help you sort out some names before then.

Josiah was a good king who instituted reforms in Judah, cleansing the land from idols and putting the Word of God back in its rightful place. He died, however, fighting against Pharaoh Neco of Egypt in a battle at Megiddo in 609 BC. Neco was on his way to aid the Assyrians against the Babylonians at a place called Carchemish.

The people of Judah made Josiah's son Jehoahaz king (also called Shallum), but Neco came to Jerusalem and deposed him after three months' reign and placed his brother Eliakim on the throne, renaming him Jehoiakim.

After defeating the Assyrians and Egyptians at Carchemish in 605 BC, Nebuchadnezzar and the Babylonian army came against Jehoiakim, taking captive some of the young nobles, including Daniel. Jehoiakim died in 597 BC, and his son Jehoiachin (also called Jeconiah and Coniah) became king.

After a reign of only three months, Jehoiachin was taken to Babylon in 597 BC along with Ezekiel and 10,000 other captives. Nebuchadnezzar installed his uncle Mattaniah (Jehoiakim and Jehoahaz's brother) as king and changed his name to Zedekiah. He reigned from 597 BC until the final captivity in 586 BC. You'll read about this later in Jeremiah.

So there are three main dates to remember: 605, 597, and 586 BC. Each of these involved a captivity of some of Judah by Babylon, and in the cases of 597 and 586, they marked the end of the last three kings of Judah. Jehoiakim died in 597, Jehoichin his son was taken captive, and Zedekiah was taken captive in 586.

Record a theme for Jeremiah 22 on JEREMIAH AT A GLANCE.

DAYS FOUR & FIVE

Now read Jeremiah 23, and as usual, mark the key words. Also mark references to *shepherds, priests,* and the *Branch,* and list what you learn about each. When you make lists, be sure to keep asking the 5 W's and an H. Look at each place you marked a particular word, ask the 5 W's and an H, and write down the answers to these questions. These steps will keep you focused on what the text says and help you to observe carefully. And careful observation is the basis of sound interpretation.

In historical narrative, getting the facts straight is one of the keys. Understanding how they relate to God's principles and learning more about God's character will empower us to live by these principles.

Read Isaiah 11:1-10. Does this relate to the Branch?

Read Deuteronomy 13:1-11 and 18:18-22. What did you learn about false prophets, and how does that relate to Jeremiah

22? Now read 2 Peter 2:1-3. What did you learn about false prophets, and how does that relate to today?

Finally, record the theme of Jeremiah 23 on JEREMIAH AT A GLANCE.

DAY SIX

Our last chapter for the week is very short, so we can spend a little more time making sure we understand it. Read Jeremiah 24 through without marking anything but the time reference. Check this against THE RULERS AND PROPHETS OF JEREMIAH'S TIME in the appendix.

Read the chapter again, this time marking the two kinds of figs. Now list what you learn about the two kinds of figs on a side-by-side chart. What is the future of each? Now, to be sure you understand, who are the good figs? What makes them good?

Record a theme for Jeremiah 24 on JEREMIAH AT A GLANCE.

DAY SEVEN

Store in your heart: Jeremiah 23:5-6

Read and discuss: Jeremiah 21; 22:13-30; 23:1-32; 24

QUESTIONS FOR DISCUSSION OR INDIVIDUAL STUDY

~ Discuss the prophecy against each king: Zedekiah, Shallum, Jehoiakim, and Coniah. Be sure to note what they have in common—what all these kings have done.

ço Discuss the righteous Branch.

ço Discuss false prophets of Jeremiah's time and our time. Be sure to include what you learned from the cross-references. How does this apply to our time?

ço Discuss the good figs and bad figs. What makes them good or bad? What is their future? Why do you think God wants the good figs to do what He tells them?

ço What application can you make from the examples these give us?

THOUGHT FOR THE WEEK

What does it mean to be a good fig? God told Jeremiah that the good figs would prosper.

> For I will set My eyes on them for good, and I will bring them again to this land; and I will build them up and not overthrow them, and I will plant them and not pluck them up. I will give them a heart to know Me, for I am the LORD; and they will be My people, and I will be their God, for they will return to Me with their whole heart (Jeremiah 24:6-7).

These people had been idolaters! God didn't promise to prosper them because they were good people. In fact, they would go into captivity! The way to understand the good figs is to understand the bad figs.

The bad figs were rebellious against God, they were disobedient, and they did not believe God's Word sent through His prophet Jeremiah. So the rebellious, disobedient unbelievers will die by sword, famine, and pestilence, and they will become a reproach, a proverb, a taunt, and a curse. They'll be destroyed from the land God promised to their forefathers because they wouldn't listen to God in difficult times.

The immediate context and application of this idea of good and bad figs is to the people living in Jerusalem and Judah at the time of Jeremiah, but this chapter also has something to say to us. What do we expect God to do to those who are rebellious, disobedient, and unbelieving? Should they prosper, or should they suffer somehow? Our understanding of justice, of course, is that they should suffer. But is that God's justice? What did God do for you when you were rebellious, disobedient, and unbelieving? Did He make you a reproach, proverb, taunt, or curse? Or did He give you several chances?

But what if you never change? What if you remain rebellious, disobedient, and unbelieving? What then? Doesn't justice demand your destruction? It does, and that is what happens. There is a hell and eternal punishment. There is justice for the unbeliever.

It's interesting to notice here that the words *rebellious* and *disobedient* are connected to *unbelieving*. Many today claim to be believers yet remain rebellious and disobedient. God is consistent. He doesn't change. Rebellion and disobedience are not the characteristics of believers. No one is perfect, and anyone who says he has not sinned is a liar (1 John 1:6-10), so we're not talking about sinless perfection. What God does make clear is that the believer is not rebellious and disobedient *all* the time, consistently, and as a pattern of life. The one who lives this way should examine himself to see if he is in the faith, because that kind of life is characteristic of the unbeliever.

Abraham believed, and God counted it as righteousness (Genesis 15:6). But Abraham was not perfect either. No one has ever led a sinless life except Jesus; that's not what we're talking about. Rather, we are referring to the kind of evidence that 1 John describes. If you're not sure about your own life, why don't you read 1 John and then ask the Lord to show you?

WILL YOU EVER LISTEN?

Jeremiah began preaching in the thirteenth year of Josiah's reign as king of Judah. The people still wouldn't listen to him 23 years later. They preferred the messages of the false prophets. They rejected the message of difficult times, God's message through Jeremiah, and instead embraced a message of prosperity from false prophets. Accepting the truth can be so hard!

DAYS ONE, TWO, & THREE

This week we're going to take three days to observe Jeremiah 25 because of the importance of understanding this vital chapter. Let's start by marking the key words. Be sure to mark time references, and note where this chapter would be on THE RULERS AND PROPHETS OF JEREMIAH'S TIME in the appendix. And be sure to use the 5 W's and an H.

Read Jeremiah 1 again and compare it to Jeremiah 25:1-11. Remember, context is king in interpretation. We want to be sure we've got the context down for this chapter.

Now let's look at the time reference in verse 11 more closely. Read 2 Chronicles 36:21 and Leviticus 25:1-7; 26:1-6,14-15,33-35. The Bible is its own best commentary. Comparing Scripture with Scripture (cross-referencing) is a key tool in interpretation.

Now read Leviticus 26:40-45 and Daniel 9:1-19. Do you understand the 70 years of captivity?

In Jeremiah 1, God said He would bring a nation from the north to judge Israel. In Jeremiah 20, we learned that this nation is Babylon. But although Babylon was God's chosen instrument, what will He do to Babylon?

And how does Jeremiah 25:12-31 relate to Jeremiah 1:5,10? Read Jeremiah 51:41 to see who Sheshak is.

Read Revelation 14:10 and 16:19. What do you learn about the wine cup of God's wrath and how it relates to Jeremiah 25 and Babylon?

What do you learn about shepherds?

Finally, record a theme for Jeremiah 25 on JEREMIAH AT A GLANCE.

DAY FOUR

Begin your study today by reading Jeremiah 26 and marking the key words on your bookmark. Note the time references on THE RULERS AND PROPHETS OF JEREMIAH'S TIME in the appendix.

What happened to Shiloh? What does God mean about making Jerusalem like Shiloh? Read 1 Samuel 4. What departed from Israel?

How was Jeremiah threatened in this chapter? How did it turn out? Who helped him?

Finally, determine a theme for Jeremiah 26 and record it on JEREMIAH AT A GLANCE.

Ꮖ𝒜𝒴𝒮 ℱ𝒾𝒱ℰ & 𝒮𝒾𝒳

We're going to look at two chapters together because of the common message and timing. Start with Jeremiah 27. Read it and mark key words as usual. Note the time reference in verse 1 and compare it to THE RULERS AND PROPHETS OF JEREMIAH'S TIME.

What visual aid does Jeremiah use in this chapter, and what does it represent? Recall he's used a linen waistband, the potter's wheel and pot, and a clay pot to make points earlier in the book.

A yoke is most often associated with carrying a burden, but it also can refer to the yoke of slavery. From the context here, we see that the yoke of serving Nebuchadnezzar king of Babylon means slavery.

What do you learn about the vessels of the temple and the prophets in verses 16-22?

Think about what you have learned. Is there any application here? If so, what?

Now read Jeremiah 28, marking key words, including *yoke*. Note the time phrase in verse 1 and compare it to 27:1. How do chapters 27 and 28 relate?

Record themes for Jeremiah 27 and 28 on JEREMIAH AT A GLANCE.

Ꮧ𝒜𝒴 𝒮ℰ𝒱ℰ𝒩

 Store in your heart: Jeremiah 27:5

Read and discuss: Jeremiah 25:1-17,34-38; 26; 27; 28

QUESTIONS FOR DISCUSSION OR INDIVIDUAL STUDY

- ∽ Discuss what you learn about judgment: whom God judges, how, and why. Include what you learned about the wine cup of the wrath of God.

- ∽ Do you think your country will be judged? Explain your answer using Scripture.

- ∽ Discuss the plot to kill Jeremiah and compare it to what God told Jeremiah in chapter 1.

- ∽ Discuss what you learned about the usage of the word *yoke* in chapters 27 and 28. Include the visual aid Jeremiah used.

- ∽ What happened to the false prophet Hananiah, and why? What will happen to the kings, the temple, and the vessels of the temple? How does this episode compare to previous chapters?

- ∽ Be sure to leave time for your group to share application in their lives.

THOUGHT FOR THE WEEK

God chose Israel to be His own treasured possession. After Solomon's reign, the nation split into two kingdoms, and 200 years after that, Assyria took the northern kingdom (Israel) into captivity because of Israel's idolatry. The southern kingdom (Judah) could not accept the idea that God would do the same to them. They clung to the promise of God's presence in Jerusalem at the temple Solomon built, and they rejected anyone who said that captivity was coming. They rejected the message that going to captivity was obedience to God. They might have heard Jeremiah speaking, but they wouldn't listen.

God warned them that they would serve Babylon for 70

years. He also said He would make Jerusalem like Shiloh—physically and spiritually destroyed, torn down and without God's glory.

Even more difficult to take was subjugation to another nation, an idolatrous nation—Babylon. How could God use such a people as His instrument against His *chosen* people, Israel? And here is an important truth. God establishes nations. He establishes rulers in those nations and uses them for His purposes. And God also expects all nations to acknowledge this. When they are idolatrous, not acknowledging Him as God, He has a case against them, a controversy with them, and is fully justified in judging them.

In Jeremiah 25, God says He will judge all the nations around Judah, and He names them. They will serve Babylon for the same 70 years. But although God uses Babylon as His instrument of judgment on them, He will also judge Babylon itself. At the end of those 70 years, God will use another nation to judge Babylon. God rules over *all* nations.

But this judgment on the nations is not just at the time of Jeremiah. God's wrath is not satisfied by what happened in the days of Jeremiah, Ezekiel, and Daniel. God's wrath will be poured out at a later time, when all nations are finally judged, as His prophets have declared from the days of Jeremiah and before, right through to Revelation.

And why does God pour out His wrath on the nations? Because they won't listen to the message of His prophets that He is the one and only God who created them and who deserves their obedience.

Upon entering the promised land, Judah stood on Mounts Ebal and Gerazim, reciting the blessings and curses God promised for obedience and disobedience. Israel was to be a light to the nations, showing them who God is and what a covenant relationship with Him brings. They failed because they turned to idols. They didn't live according to the covenant.

The church has that mission today. Our role is to show the world how to live and love according to God's Word and what happens when we do. And though we might not experience the kind of prosperity the world seeks, we are to reflect the richness of our relationship to the Lord, even in difficult times.

I Will Restore Your Fortunes

ᘜᘜᘜᘜ

God will judge Judah for their idolatry and for not listening to Him. They will suffer famine, sword, pestilence, the destruction of Jerusalem and the temple, and 70 years of captivity in Babylon. Is that the end? Or will God do something else? Remember, God keeps His promises.

Day One

We're more than halfway through our quest to understand Jeremiah! Hang in there on this exciting journey.

Today, read Jeremiah 29 and mark the key words as you have been doing. This chapter contains several messages by letters, so paying attention to the audience and message of each will help you understand the chapter. Mark the key phrase *restore your fortunes*[12] and add it to your bookmark. Similar phrases occur in later chapters.

Other messages were being delivered to the people of Jerusalem and Judah. How are they characterized in this chapter? Which messages do the people listen to and trust in?

Read the following and think about the days of Jeremiah and today:

Matthew 24:24-25

John 8:44

Acts 20:28-31

2 Timothy 3:1-8,13

2 Timothy 4:1-4

2 Peter 2:1-3

If you've got the time, also read these passages:

John 14:16-17,26

John 16:13-15

1 John 4:1-4

Jude 3-4

Record a theme for Jeremiah 29 on JEREMIAH AT A GLANCE.

DAY TWO

Read through Jeremiah 30 and mark the key words. Don't miss the time phrases.

Let's look more closely at the *time of Jacob's distress.*[13] List what you learn about it. Use the 5 W's and an H. Who is it for? What will happen? When will it occur? How does it relate to restoration? Who will be their leader?

God gave us prophecy not so we could make charts and timelines, but so we could better understand His character and ways. This event does fit into a prophetic timeline, and to understand it fully, you'll need to cross-reference passages from Ezekiel, Daniel, Joel, Matthew, and others. That is more than we can take on in this series, so let's focus on God's character.

Compare this message with what we've seen so far in Jeremiah. Compare the message of judgment with this message. This will be a good topic for discussion this week.

Record the theme for Jeremiah 30 on JEREMIAH AT A GLANCE.

DAYS THREE & FOUR

Read Jeremiah 31, and as usual, mark the key words. This chapter is one of the most important in the Bible, so we're going to take two days to cover it.

Don't miss *covenant*, which we recommend you always mark in every book of the Bible. It's key wherever you find it. Many other terms are related to *covenant*, such as *lovingkindness*,[14] which refers to God's faithful love that is based on His covenant with us.

Note the time phrase that starts the chapter. How does that connect chapters 30 and 31?

You might want to mark *joy* and its synonyms in Jeremiah 31 because these convey a good sense of the message of this chapter.

Now let's look more closely at verses 31-33. List what you learn about *covenant*.

Next, look up the following and think about their connections:

Ezekiel 36:22-28

Luke 22:1,7-8,14-20

Hebrews 8:6-13

Hebrews 9:11-22

So who is included in this new covenant promised to Israel

and Jacob? Read Ephesians 2:11-18. Is the promise still valid for Israel? Read Romans 11:1-2,11-12,25-29 and compare to Jeremiah 31:35-40.

Finally, record the theme for Jeremiah 31 on JEREMIAH AT A GLANCE.

DAYS FIVE & SIX

Read Jeremiah 32, marking the key words on your bookmark, geographical references, and time indicators. You'll meet a character named Baruch in this chapter. He is significant in a few later chapters, so you might want to mark him and add him to your bookmark.

Review Jeremiah 1:1. Where is Jeremiah from?

List what you learn about the deed of purchase, which is first mentioned in verse 10. What is to be done and why?

What do you learn about God in this chapter? There are a few verses you may recognize from praise music.

The events in this chapter occurred much later than the events of previous chapters. How does this chapter relate to them?

Notice how Jeremiah questions God, asking why he is to buy the land the Babylonians have captured. What is God's response to Jeremiah?

List the connections between judgment and restoration. Why the judgment? Why the restoration?

What do you learn about God that will help you in your life?

Well, that's it for this week, Beloved! Don't forget to record the theme for Jeremiah 32 on JEREMIAH AT A GLANCE.

⚬⚬⚬⚬
Day Seven

Store in your heart: Jeremiah 32:17

Read and discuss: Jeremiah 29:1-14,30-32; 30:5-11,17-22; 31; 32:16-27,36-44

Questions for Discussion or Individual Study

- ⚬ What did you learn this week about truth and lies? Discuss the New Testament perspective. What does this imply we need to do?

- ⚬ Discuss the restoration the Lord promises Israel amid all the judgment and distress you've seen so far in Jeremiah. Is there any application to your life?

- ⚬ Discuss "the time of Jacob's distress" (or trouble).

- ⚬ Discuss the new covenant, including the references to the cross.

- ⚬ What are the connections between judgment and restoration?

- ⚬ What did you learn about God this week that will help you in your walk? How does it affect your confidence even when you don't understand what's going on around you?

Thought for the Week

The new covenant God promised Israel is key to the promise of restoration. The nation is undergoing judgment because they broke the covenant of the Law made at Mount Sinai. They worshipped other gods, made images, and bowed down to them. They took the Lord's name in vain, they did not keep the Sabbath holy, and they did not love the Lord their God with all their heart, soul, mind, and strength. Neither did they love their neighbors as themselves.

So what is God to do with such a people? Because of His covenant with Abraham, God promised to make a new covenant, not like the one He made at Mount Sinai with their forefathers when He brought Israel out of Egypt, which they broke. This one will be based on a better promise, with a better high priest, a better sacrifice, and better blood.

God enacted this new covenant with the blood of His own Son, who willingly became flesh and dwelled among us, yet without sin. He was made sin for us, bearing all our sins as the sacrifice in our place, substituting for us, shedding His blood to atone for our sins.

At the same time, He became the great High Priest, taking His own blood and sprinkling it on the real, true, heavenly mercy seat—not the representative copy made on earth. He Himself, in His torn flesh at the crucifixion, tore apart the veil that separated worshippers from the presence of God. Now those in this covenant can enter boldly, approaching the throne of grace themselves, without fear of death because of Christ's substitutionary, propitiatory, atoning death. This is the promise to those in the new covenant.

But is this just for Israel and Judah? What about those of us who are Gentiles? We were not part of the covenant of the Law. Did we break it? Did we deserve death? The Scripture declares that yes, we did. We were without hope and without God in the world. But we who were far off have now been drawn near. In addition, those in the old covenant and those of us who were not under the law were formerly separated by the law, but Christ broke down this barrier in His flesh by His blood. Now the two are made into one new man, reconciled through the cross. And thus we have peace with God.

In this new relationship, we are not powerless to obey. God removes our heart of stone, gives us a new heart, and writes His law on our new heart of flesh. He gives us His Spirit to dwell in us and to empower us to listen to Him and obey at all times, even difficult ones. His strength in us keeps us faithful when there seems to be no hope. God the Holy Spirit in us convicts us of our wrong thinking and actions, enables us to choose rightly, and empowers us to live in a manner that is worthy of our calling.

All this is the grace of God, freely given in love. For God loved us before we loved Him, and while we were sinners, Christ died for us. Before the foundation of the world God chose us in Christ that we would be holy and blameless before Him.

What a God! What love! What a future and hope for Israel!

A Righteous Branch

What is it like to be ruled by someone who is righteous? Judah didn't have much experience with that. Only a few kings listened to the Lord in good times or difficult times. Zedekiah and Jehoiakim certainly didn't listen. And they weren't even close to righteous. Would Israel ever have a righteous ruler?

Days One & Two

Today and tomorrow we'll look at Jeremiah 33. Let's start by marking the key words from your bookmark.

Make sure you catch the timing of this chapter. Look back at Jeremiah 32:1-3. Note from 33:1-5 what is going on in Jerusalem.

What does God say He will do? Take your time on this assignment.

Now what does God say about the *Branch of David?*

We trust you marked *covenant.* What covenant is this? Read 2 Samuel 7:8-16; 2 Chronicles 13:5; 21:7; and Psalm 89:3-4,28-29.

What else will be permanent? Read Malachi 2:1-9. Observe it carefully, marking *covenant.* What do you learn about the Levitical priests?

Be sure to record the theme of Jeremiah 33 on JEREMIAH AT A GLANCE.

Finally, how does the phrase *restore their fortunes* connect chapters 29–33? Check your JEREMIAH AT A GLANCE chart for help.

Days Three & Four

The more you read Jeremiah, considering his message and meditating on truth, the better you will understand your God. And when you consider our own times, you'll see why He has you studying this book now.

Read Jeremiah 34, marking the key words from your bookmark. Remember to note time phrases and refer to THE RULERS AND PROPHETS OF JEREMIAH'S TIME in the appendix. Also review the historical summary on pages 54–55. The chapters of Jeremiah are arranged thematically, not chronologically. But chapters 25 and following include many references to the kings, so you can see when these events occur. Knowing the historical background will help. For example, this chapter is in the reign of which king? What has happened before?

Covenant is key again here in chapter 34. Be sure to list in your notebook what you learn about it. Also, read Genesis 15:1-21. What do you see there that is parallel to what you see in Jeremiah 34:18-19? "Made a covenant" is usually *karath berith* in the Hebrew, meaning to *cut* covenant. How do these passages help you understand that term?

Genesis 15 is a key chapter in the Bible because of what it teaches about covenant, faith, and righteousness. What do you learn about each of these in Genesis 15?

Now read Galatians 3:6-18. We don't want you to miss

this nugget! Note Genesis 15:6 in the margin of your Bible at Galatians 3:6 and vice versa. These passages are critical.

If you have time, read the rest of Galatians 3 about the relationship between the Law and promise.

Record the theme of Jeremiah 34 on JEREMIAH AT A GLANCE.

Day Five

Today's assignment is Jeremiah 35. As usual, as you read, mark the key words from your bookmark.

Outline the basic story of the Rechabites. What was the command, what was the temptation, and what was their response?

Now what was God's Word to the Rechabites based on their behavior? What principle was God trying to show Judah? What application of this principle can you make to your own life?

Record the theme of Jeremiah 35 on JEREMIAH AT A GLANCE.

Day Six

Our last chapter for the week is Jeremiah 36. We'll see Baruch again, so be sure to mark his name along with the key words from your bookmark.

This is historical narrative, so getting the story down is important. Note the major characters and their actions or responses to others' actions. Keep asking the 5 W's and an H. The text answers them.

God told Israel in Exodus 12:2 that their first month would

be in the spring, when the first feast, Passover, occurs. So the ninth month of the Hebrew year corresponds to November–December, when Jerusalem is quite cold and sometimes sees snow.

What is Jehoiakim's attitude toward God's words? How does this reflect his attitude toward Jeremiah as God's spokesman?

What does God say will happen because of Jehoiakim's actions regarding the scroll?

Record the theme of Jeremiah 36 on JEREMIAH AT A GLANCE.

DAY SEVEN

 Store in your heart: Jeremiah 33:16

Read and discuss: Jeremiah 33–34; 35:18; 36

QUESTIONS FOR DISCUSSION OR INDIVIDUAL STUDY

- ∾ Discuss what you learned from the days of Zedekiah about releasing Hebrew bondservants.

- ∾ What did you learn in Jeremiah and the cross-references about covenants?

- ∾ What did you learn about God, His character, and His ways?

- ∾ What is the bottom line about the Rechabites that you can apply to your life?

- ∾ What lessons did you learn from the story about Jehoiakim burning the scroll?

Thought for the Week

The story of Zedekiah and the release of the captives reinforces a key principle that's taught elsewhere in Scripture: Partial obedience is disobedience.

The covenant of the Law demanded that if a Hebrew became a bondservant to another Hebrew, he should be released after seven years. Israel had not followed that command. Recently, Judah had declared release of their neighbors. From all that's transpired in Jeremiah, one can imagine that they had heard Jeremiah's message, had seen two captivities, and were looking for some relief from the impending disaster as Nebuchadnezzar was at the walls. After all, hadn't Hezekiah turned to the Lord for relief from Assyrian assault?

But Zedekiah and the people simply wanted relief. They didn't obey God from their hearts when they covenanted with God to release their Hebrew servants, although they followed the letter of their promise. They released them, but then they took them back. They did not follow the intent of the Law, which was freedom for those Hebrews for that time on.

Saul made the same kind of mistake in 1 Samuel 15. God had told Saul to kill all the Amalekites, including their livestock, but he left their king, Agag, alive, as well as the best of the flocks and herds. When challenged by Samuel about his disobedience to God, Saul's excuse was that the *people* did this and that these animals would be used to sacrifice to God. This was Samuel's reply to Saul:

> Has the LORD as much delight in burnt offerings
>   and sacrifices
> As in obeying the voice of the LORD?
> Behold, to obey is better than sacrifice,
> And to heed than the fat of rams.
> For rebellion is as the sin of divination,

And insubordination is as iniquity and idolatry.
Because you have rejected the word of the LORD,
He has also rejected you from being king
(1 Samuel 15:22-23).

Saul met his end on Mount Gilboa at the hands of the Philistines, and David became king.

Zedekiah will be given into the hands of his enemies, the army of the king of Babylon, which had temporarily left the siege to counter another military threat. He will not die by the sword, but he will die in captivity, no longer the king of Judah. He would be the last king of Judah, for after the return from captivity in 536 BC, there were only governors under the Persians, then the Greeks, and then the Romans. These other nations installed their own kings, none of whom was from the house of David.

Zedekiah died in captivity, and the rule of the descendants of David ended for a long time. But this situation won't last forever because God made a covenant with David, and one day, a Branch will arise and rule in righteousness.

LEADERSHIP CAN MAKE OR BREAK A NATION

~~~~~~~~~

Josiah, Jehoahaz, Jehoiakim, Jehoiachin, Zedekiah—the final kings of Judah before Nebuchadnezzar destroyed Jerusalem. Who led the country well? Who led them into disaster, destruction, and captivity? Who listened to God? Who refused to listen? Leadership can make or break a nation.

DAY ONE

Read Jeremiah 37 and mark the key words from your bookmark. Although we haven't had you mark *siege*[15] so far, it's important in the historical narrative and in Jeremiah's message. You can decide if you want to mark it. Be sure to notice the words that refer to the same thing.

Note the sequence of events in your notebook.

Did Jeremiah's message come true? What was the test of a prophet? When was Jeremiah accused of going over to the enemy—before or after his message was confirmed?

Read Jeremiah 29 again and note the similar circumstances—the king, when in his reign these events occur, the accusations, and the opposition. Remember, Jeremiah has been prophesying since the thirteenth year of Josiah's reign, so by this point, he's been delivering unpleasant news for 30 years.

Notice Zedekiah's request in verse 3. Is this consistent with his not listening to Jeremiah? Do you know anyone who acts like Zedekiah?

Record the theme of Jeremiah 37 on JEREMIAH AT A GLANCE.

DAY TWO

Read Jeremiah 38 today, marking key words and phrases from your bookmark. Again, note the sequence of events in your notebook.

Who came to Jeremiah's defense? What is Zedekiah's response to him?

When Jeremiah gives Zedekiah God's word again, what does Zedekiah want him to do? What is Jeremiah's fate?

Record the theme of Jeremiah 38 on JEREMIAH AT A GLANCE.

DAYS THREE & FOUR

Read Jeremiah 39 today and mark the key words and phrases from your bookmark. Note the time phrases and list the sequence of events in your notebook. What happened to the Ethiopian eunuch? What happened to Jeremiah?

Create a three-column chart and compare Jeremiah 39 with 2 Kings 25:1-22 and 2 Chronicles 36:11-17.

Record the theme of Jeremiah 39 on JEREMIAH AT A GLANCE.

DAYS FIVE & SIX

Read Jeremiah 40–41, marking the key words and phrases as usual. Again, note the time phrases and geographical references. List the characters and the events. Review Jeremiah 39:14.

Record the themes of Jeremiah 40–41 on JEREMIAH AT A GLANCE.

DAY SEVEN

 Store in your heart: Jeremiah 38:20
Read and discuss: Jeremiah 37–41

QUESTIONS FOR DISCUSSION OR INDIVIDUAL STUDY

- ∾ Discuss the sequence of events in these chapters and your insights about Jeremiah: what happened to him, why, and how it all relates to Jeremiah 1.

- ∾ Discuss Zedekiah's relationship to Jeremiah and to the Lord.

- ∾ Review Jeremiah 24—the good and bad figs—and relate that to Jeremiah 39.

- ∾ Discuss the Ethiopian eunuch's role and future.

- ∾ What is the intention of the remnant in the land?

- ∾ What application is there in this lesson for your life?

Thought for the Week

Leadership can make or break a nation. Joash was seven years old when he became king around 835 BC. He decided to restore the temple because it had been defiled with idols and neglected.

Joash, with Jehoiada the priest, returned Judah to right worship. But when Jehoiada died, Joash listened to the officials of the people, and they returned to idolatry. God sent prophets to them to bring them back to Him, including Obadiah and Joel, but they would not listen. When Jehoiada's son Zedekiah called the people into account over their idolatry, Joash ordered him killed.

More than 100 years later, Hezekiah became king, and in the first year of his reign he opened the doors of the temple and repaired them. He called the Levites to cleanse the temple of idols, to rebuild the utensils that had been destroyed, and to restore proper worship. With Isaiah the prophet, Hezekiah turned to the Lord for help against the Assyrians, who were turned away.

About another 100 years later, another boy king arose: Josiah. When he was 16, he began to seek the Lord. And when he was 20, he began to purge the idols from Judah and Jerusalem. Then when he was 26 and had finished purging the land, he began to repair the temple. And in the process, Hilkiah the priest found the book of the Law, which had been lost in the temple. Josiah had Jeremiah and Zephaniah to help with the reforms. But did the people really listen?

So the people of Judah experienced "revivals" in the days of Joash, Hezekiah, and Josiah. But when the godly leaders died, the people returned to their former ways. They did not listen to the prophets God sent, nor did they embrace the reforms each of these leaders instituted. Before and after each of these kings, the people worshipped idols. As Peter quoted in his second letter, "'A dog returns to its own vomit,' and, 'A sow, after washing, returns to wallowing in the mire.'"

The people never really changed. These leaders instituted reforms, including cleaning, repairing, and restoring the temple and its utensils and furniture. But the hearts of the people never changed. As soon as the godly leaders died, the people returned to their ways like a dog returns to its own vomit. They had never changed.

Many people are the same today. They get excited when a dynamic leader challenges them to reform. They see the benefit at the time, but when that leadership is gone, they revert to their former state because they haven't really changed inside. What they need is a spiritual heart transplant. Prophets can point out what's wrong and the path to correct it. Leaders can direct people on that path. But without leaders, people stray from the path and return to their former lives.

That's the challenge Moses faced. While he was on the mountain, the people built a golden calf and returned to idolatry. They longed for Egypt and slavery, where they had plenty of food, and they were unwilling to face the hardship of walking the path to the promised land of Canaan. Only a strong leader can keep people pointed in the right direction.

So who did Judah have for leaders after Josiah was killed? Jehoahaz, Jehoiakim, Jehoiachin, and Zedekiah. Which of them listened to the Lord? Which of them led the people on the right path, away from idolatry and toward God? Which of them understood that the exile to Babylon was God's will and would lead to restoration? None.

Did these kings lack God's messenger? No. Did they lack godly examples of kings before them to follow? No. Leadership matters. It can make or break a nation.

Are You Seeking Great Things for Yourself?

What do you seek after? Peace? Safety? Happiness? Contentment? Satisfaction? Honor? Material possessions? What does God say about that?

Days One & Two

Read Jeremiah 42 today, marking key words and phrases from your bookmark. Outline the sequence of events and the message from the Lord. Note the promises made before the message. What would happen if the people listened to Jeremiah's message? What would happen if they didn't? How does this compare with God's promise to the people in Jerusalem before the captivity to Babylon (Jeremiah 24)?

Record the theme of Jeremiah 42 on JEREMIAH AT A GLANCE.

Day Three

Read Jeremiah 43, marking key words and phrases from your bookmark. Don't miss the geographical references.

The narrative continues. How does it relate to chapter 42? Note the people's reaction to the message and contrast it to the promise they made when they requested Jeremiah to inquire of God on their behalf (42:5-6).

What was the message from God?

Why did the people flee to Egypt? Could Egypt protect them from Nebuchadnezzar?

Record the theme of Jeremiah 43 on JEREMIAH AT A GLANCE.

DAYS FOUR & FIVE

Read Jeremiah 44, marking key words as usual. Be sure to mark geographical locations.

Again, outline the messages from God and the people's reaction. What are they saying about Jeremiah?

The people didn't believe Jeremiah's words. They needed a sign. What is the sign that they should understand? What had God just said in the previous verses? How does this—the need for signs instead of a word from the Lord—relate to people who heard Jesus or Paul? How does it relate to people who hear the Word of God today?

Record the theme of Jeremiah 44 on JEREMIAH AT A GLANCE.

DAY SIX

Read and mark the key words and phrases of Jeremiah 45 today. Don't miss the timing or the main character.

Read Jeremiah 32; 36; and 43 to review what you learned

about Baruch. Look at the time phrases and list the events in chronological order.

What is Baruch's situation? How does it relate to Jeremiah 36? Next week we'll consider why this message might have been placed in this position—between the story concluded in Jeremiah 44 and the prophecy beginning in Jeremiah 46.

Record the theme of Jeremiah 45 on JEREMIAH AT A GLANCE.

DAY SEVEN

 Store in your heart: Jeremiah 42:6
Read and discuss: Jeremiah 42–44

QUESTIONS FOR DISCUSSION OR INDIVIDUAL STUDY

∞ Discuss the sequence of events in chapters 42–44. Take your time and discuss this thoroughly.

∞ Now discuss Jeremiah 44:15-19. Relate this to what has been happening all through Jeremiah. Don't miss the people's attitude and their accusations against Jeremiah. Does this happen today?

∞ Discuss Jeremiah 44:24-29 and the need for signs instead of the word of the Lord. What signs had God performed in Egypt before? Allow time for discussion of what your group knows about this issue in the time of Jesus. Does this happen today?

∞ Review what you know about Baruch in Jeremiah. What is the significance of his quest for great things for himself? Can you apply the principle here to yourself?

Thought for the Week

Baruch was a scribe. In the fourth year of Jehoiakim's reign (605 BC), he wrote on a scroll all that Jeremiah dictated—most likely all of the book of Jeremiah to that point. At Jeremiah's direction, he read the scroll to the people in the temple on a fast day. He read it again to the king's officials. This happened in Jehoiakim's fifth year, so the first captivity had already taken place. Daniel and other young nobles had been taken to Babylon. The Babylonians had left, but the people still wouldn't listen to God. So Baruch had to hide from the king.

When the king cut up and burned the scroll, Baruch and Jeremiah hid from the king's wrath. During this time, Baruch again wrote all Jeremiah dictated, including many similar words.

In Jeremiah 45, we see that God spoke to Baruch right after he wrote all Jeremiah dictated, before he read it to the people, before the king cut up and burned the scroll, and before the king sought his life.

Baruch knew God's message to Judah—he had just written it down. What was his reaction? "Woe is me!"

What was God's response to this? Here's a paraphrase: "I'm in charge; I built it and I can tear it down. You, Baruch, should be glad you get to live. You have your life; don't seek great things for yourself."

This message came more than 600 years before Jesus' three-year earthly ministry, which included His famous Sermon on the Mount. Jesus preached the same message in different words: Seek *first* the kingdom of God and His righteousness.

Matthew 6 reminds us that treasures on earth are unimportant. They can be destroyed or stolen, but treasures in heaven last forever. Therefore, Jesus taught us not to worry about tomorrow or about what we'll eat or drink or wear. "Where your treasure is, there your heart will be also."

The temptation to Baruch and to us is to say "woe is me" when things don't go well, when we see terrible things on the horizon. When our society is full of evil, when tough economic times come, when geological or meteorological disasters occur, when life is difficult…at times like these, we need to listen to God's Word.

Our first priority is to seek God, His kingdom, and His righteousness, not food or clothing. God provides those for us. He wants our hearts.

Jeremiah's contemporaries in Judah had a hard time listening to God because of His message of judgment. People are no different today. No one wants to hear a message of judgment. But God judges sin, and your nation is not exempt. God will not be mocked. Judgment is coming. Times will be difficult, and you will be tempted to focus on temporal concerns, but God's incarnate Word said, "seek first His kingdom." He also said this:

> If anyone wishes to come after Me, he must deny himself, and take up his cross and follow Me. For whoever wishes to save his life will lose it; but whoever loses his life for My sake will find it. For what will it profit a man if he gains the whole world and forfeits his soul? Or what will a man give in exchange for his soul? For the Son of Man is going to come in the glory of His Father with His angels, and will then repay every man according to his deeds (Matthew 16:24-27).

WHY ARE THE NATIONS IN AN UPROAR?

ᠬᠥᠬᠥ

God addresses the kings, whom He calls the "judges (or leaders) of the earth," in this way: "Do homage to the Son, that He not become angry, and you perish in the way" (Psalm 2:12a). Although this message was given thousands of years ago, rulers today would do well to heed its warning.

DAY ONE

As you'll see, the next four chapters are prophecies to the nations. Review what you learned in Jeremiah 1 about Jeremiah's call and commission. (If you don't remember, read Jeremiah 1:4-12.) Now read Jeremiah 46, marking the key words and phrases from your bookmark. Make sure to note each nation addressed. Mark geographical references and compare THE NATIONS OF JEREMIAH'S PROPHECY in the appendix.

Notice the time phrase in verse 2. It doesn't set the timing of the chapter, but it specifies the army.

In the case of each prophecy, note who is being judged, why, and who is bringing the judgment. Also make note of any hope for Israel. The name *LORD of Hosts* or *Lord GOD of Hosts*[16] indicates His power in the host of His armies in heaven.

Record the theme of Jeremiah 46 on JEREMIAH AT A GLANCE.

DAY TWO

Read Jeremiah 47 today, marking key words and phrases. It's short.

Caphtor is the place the Philistines migrated from when they settled along the coast of what is Israel today. Gaza and Ashkelon exist today on the Mediterranean coast. If you're not familiar with the relationship of the Philistines to Israel, remember that Samson fought the Philistines until Delilah betrayed him (Judges 13–16). Goliath, whom David killed, was a Philistine (1 Samuel 17). Saul died in battle with the Philistines on Mount Gilboa (1 Samuel 31; 1 Chronicles 10). These and other stories illustrate how the Philistines plagued Israel from the time they entered Canaan until David subdued them. If you're not familiar with these events, read the selected chapters.

Record the theme of Jeremiah 46 on JEREMIAH AT A GLANCE.

Since chapter 46 is so short, now is a good time to reflect on the placement of chapter 45. The story is about Baruch, and it occurs in the fourth year of Jehoiakim. But chapters 37 through 44 are a sequential historical narrative from the reign of Zedekiah through the last captivity, as some of the remnant fled to Egypt. Why would God place the message of Jeremiah 45 right before these prophecies against the nations?

DAYS THREE & FOUR

Let's take two days to cover Jeremiah 48 because it's so long. Read it and mark the key words and phrases from your bookmark as usual. Watch especially for geographical locations, which you can locate on THE NATIONS OF JEREMIAH'S PROPHECY in the appendix.

Read Genesis 19:29-38 for the origin of Moab. Lot is Abraham's nephew. Israel and Moab share many other connections as well. For example, Ruth, who became part of the royal bloodline, was a Moabitess. But relations were not usually friendly because Moab worshipped Chemosh, not God.

Take your time and note what Moab is being punished for and how. Also look for any hope in the chapter. Read Jeremiah 12:14-17 and Daniel 11:36-41.

Timing is key in these prophecies. Don't miss the time phrases.

Record the theme of Jeremiah 48 on JEREMIAH AT A GLANCE.

Days Five & Six

We'll spend another two days on one long chapter. As you observe Jeremiah 49, mark references to the nations being judged. Again, each of these has a long relationship with Israel.

You've already seen Ammon's origin. If you're not familiar with Edom, read Genesis 25:19-34. (Jacob later is called Israel.) Also read Obadiah for insight into Moab's judgment.

Check THE NATIONS OF JEREMIAH'S PROPHECY in the appendix for the locations of the others mentioned. Damascus is the capital of Syria today, or Aram as it's sometimes called in the Old Testament. Hazor is not the city in Galilee; rather, with Kedar it's thought to be a nomadic people in the desert east of Israel toward the Persian Gulf, south of Babylon. Elam is north of the Persian Gulf, on the border between Iraq and Iran today.

You can also check Bible dictionaries for more information about these nations.

Finally, record the theme of Jeremiah 49 on JEREMIAH AT A GLANCE.

Day Seven

Store in your heart: Jeremiah 46:28

Read and discuss: Jeremiah 46–49 (don't read all the verses of these long chapters)

Questions for Discussion or Individual Study

- ∾ Start by discussing Jeremiah's call and commission as well as God's promise to watch over His word to perform it.

- ∾ Why do you think chapter 45 is positioned right before these chapters? What is its relationship to the prophecies about the nations?

- ∾ Discuss the judgment on each nation, chapter by chapter, using the 5 W's and an H. Cover the origin and relationship of each nation to Israel as you have time. Watch your time so you can cover them all.

Thought for the Week

God's judgment of the nations isn't found only in Jeremiah. Obadiah prophesied against Edom. Jonah and Nahum prophesied against Nineveh (the capitol of Assyria). And throughout the other prophets, judgment is declared for two basic reasons. The first is idolatry—the nations' failure to worship God. The second is their treatment of Israel.

God made a covenant with Israel to be their God and to take them for His people. He would marry Israel, but she would commit adultery with other gods. Israel would break the first three commandments repeatedly. They took other gods, made images, and took God's name in vain. They deserved punishment for breaking the covenant.

But what about the nations? They had no covenant relationship with God, did they? No, they didn't, but they were to worship God anyway. Romans 1:18-32 makes clear that all mankind is accountable to God because He made Himself evident to all in the creation. But the nations suppressed the truth in unrighteousness, they did not honor Him as God, and they worshipped images (the creation) rather than the Creator.

They exchanged the glory of God for an image of creatures, and therefore He gave them over in the lusts of their heart to impurity. They exchanged the truth for a lie, and in serving the creature rather than the Creator, God gave them over to degrading passions wherein they exchanged the natural for the unnatural (homosexuality). And He gave them over to a depraved mind to commit all sorts of unrighteousness, including murder, greed, and adultery. They became haters of God, unloving, untrustworthy, and unmerciful. And they gave hearty approval to those who did the same.

But the nations are without excuse before God because God made Himself evident to them. All men, everywhere. No one is excepted.

And what about the nations' treatment of God's people, Israel? In Matthew 25, Jesus taught that when He returns, He will sit on His glorious throne, and all the nations will be gathered before Him. Here He will separate them like a shepherd separates sheep and goats. Those who treated His brothers well will inherit eternal life—the kingdom prepared for them from the foundation of the world. Those who mistreated His brothers will enter eternal punishment.

Who are Jesus' brothers? Israel. The nations, the Gentiles, are judged by how they act toward Israel. Surely Moab, Ammon, Edom, and the rest are without excuse. What about you? What about your nation? Will there be judgment? Yes. What will the outcome be?

The Judgment of Babylon

～～～～

Jeremiah not only recorded the judgment of Babylon but also sent it to Babylon and then had the scroll thrown into the Euphrates, where it sank. Then he had the messenger say, "so shall Babylon sink down and not rise again." In Revelation 18:21, an angel took a stone and threw it into the sea, saying, "So will Babylon, the great city, be thrown down with violence, and will not be found any longer."

Days One & Two

We're on our last week, faithful, diligent student! We've spent three months together gleaning truths from God's Word through Jeremiah, and we're proud of you for sticking with it. By now you know the blessings of regular time in the Scripture.

So here we go—our last three chapters. Read Jeremiah 50, marking key words and phrases from your bookmark as usual.

Record the theme of Jeremiah 50 on JEREMIAH AT A GLANCE.

DAYS THREE & FOUR

Read Jeremiah 51 through and mark key words and phrases. Watch for references to time.

Record the theme of Jeremiah 51 on JEREMIAH AT A GLANCE.

DAY FIVE

Babylon is one of the most important nations in the Bible, and its judgment occupies these two chapters and many more. For insight, read Revelation 14:8 and Revelation 17–18. To keep your time interactive, mark *Babylon*. Remember to keep asking the 5 W's and an H as you mark.

Placing all this into a well-developed end-times scenario is much too complicated for this brief survey of Jeremiah. Nevertheless, we want you to understand what the Scripture says. When you've finished with Revelation 17–18, if you're not familiar with the rest of Revelation, read it. We think you'll have to study Revelation too! And Daniel, and many others.

DAY SIX

Jeremiah ends with a historical wrap-up. Read Jeremiah 52 and mark the key words and phrases from your bookmark. Compare this chapter with Jeremiah 39; 2 Kings 25; and 2 Chronicles 36 for historical details. You might make a four-column chart to do this.

Record the theme of Jeremiah 52 on JEREMIAH AT A GLANCE. And finally, determine a theme for the book of

Jeremiah and record that on JEREMIAH AT A GLANCE as well.

<hr />

Day Seven

 Store in your heart: Jeremiah 50:20
Read and discuss: Jeremiah 50–52

Questions for Discussion or Individual Study

- ∾ Discuss all you've learned from Jeremiah and Revelation about the judgment of Babylon.

- ∾ Discuss what you've learned in Jeremiah, Kings, and Chronicles about the destruction of Jerusalem.

- ∾ What lessons have you learned in Jeremiah? What did you learn about God?

- ∾ How will you apply these lessons to your life? Leave plenty of time for this one. Make it as practical as you can.

Thought for the Week

If any theme has been consistent throughout Jeremiah, it's this: Judgment comes on those who don't listen to God and obey Him. But at the same time, Jeremiah holds out hope that if any person or any nation repents and turns to God, He will have compassion and restore their fortunes.

So we must understand why we should listen to God in difficult times. Listening to God means obeying Him. Doing what He tells us to do is the key. You have to listen, and you have to obey. Simply knowing the Scripture is not enough; you have to live it.

And when life is tough, when times are difficult, many voices compete for our attention. People have all sorts of advice. They're usually well-meaning, and their advice is often based on experience. Often, though, it's full of emotion.

And sometimes, it's absolutely the wrong advice. We have to guard against the voice that speaks to us out of malice. John 8:44 tells us that the devil has no truth in him; he is a liar and the father of lies. Peter calls him our adversary and describes him as a roaring lion who seeks to devour. John calls him the accuser of the brethren and the destroyer. His mission is to lie to us, to deceive us, to falsely accuse us, and to destroy us. And if his voice is the one we hear in the midst of difficult times, he has accomplished his mission. We'll no longer listen to God, and our lives won't be demonstrations of worship of God.

Our enemy can't take away the eternal life of believers because that's secure in Christ, but he can damage our witness. He can cause us to lose the reward that Christ gives when He comes. And that will affect our worship because our reward is meant only for us to give back to God in worship.

And if the enemy confuses us and steers us wrong in this life, we can steer others wrong. We can fail in our mission to point all men to Christ. And the judgment that falls on the lost is eternal punishment, like Babylon's punishment.

So we must listen to God. But how do we listen? First, we must know the Master's voice. Jesus described Himself as a good shepherd in John 10 and promised that His sheep would follow Him because they know His voice and would not follow the voice of a stranger. We must stay in constant contact with our Shepherd to know His voice and distinguish it from all others. We must not be like Pharaoh, who said to Moses, "Who is the LORD that I should obey His voice?" (Exodus 5:2).

How do we attend to God's voice? Through prayer and

Bible study. We must be in the Word diligently so we are able to distinguish between God's voice and voices that contradict Him. Israel lost that ability when they lost the Word of God. They strayed from hearing God and began following voices of strangers.

And if God tells us in His Word to love Him with all our hearts, all our minds, all our souls, and all our strength, we must. If He says to love our neighbor as ourselves, we must. He tells us what loving Him looks like. He tells us what a walk worthy of our calling looks like. He tells us what we must put away and stop doing and what we must do instead. And doing those things is listening to God. Even when it's difficult.

The good news is that when we believe the gospel message of Jesus, God gives us the Holy Spirit to indwell us, to empower us, and to bring to mind God's Word, which teaches us to obey. We're not helpless. We have God Himself in us, day by day, step by step. But we have to listen.

APPENDIX

Theme of Jeremiah:

Author:

Date:

Purpose:

Key Words:

SEGMENT DIVISIONS

			CHAPTER THEMES
		1	
		2	
		3	
		4	
		5	
		6	
		7	
		8	
		9	
		10	
		11	
		12	
		13	
		14	
		15	
		16	
		17	
		18	
		19	
		20	
		21	
		22	
		23	
		24	
		25	
		26	

		Chapter Themes
		27
		28
		29
		30
		31
		32
		33
		34
		35
		36
		37
		38
		39
		40
		41
		42
		43
		44
		45
		46
		47
		48
		49
		50
		51
		52

THE RULERS AND PROPHETS OF JEREMIAH'S TIME

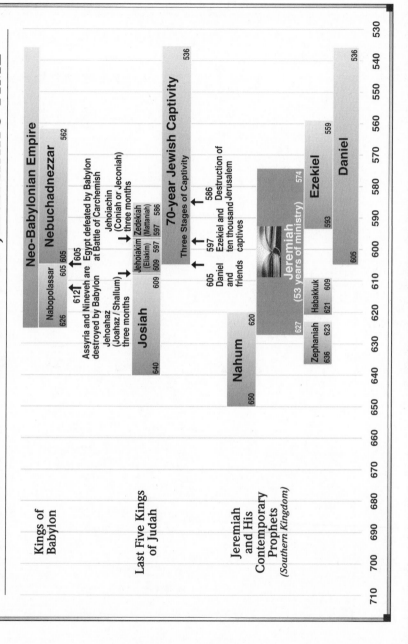

Kings of Babylon

Neo-Babylonian Empire

Nabopolassar 626 — 605

Nebuchadnezzar 605 — 562

Assyria and Nineveh are destroyed by Babylon 612

Egypt defeated by Babylon at Battle of Carchemish 605

Last Five Kings of Judah

Josiah 640 — 609

Jehoahaz (Joahaz / Shallum) three months 609

Jehoiakim (Eliakim) 609 — 597

Jehoiachin (Coniah or Jeconiah) three months 597

Zedekiah (Mattaniah) 597 — 586

70-year Jewish Captivity 586 — 536

Three Stages of Captivity

605 Daniel and friends

597 Ezekiel and ten thousand captives

586 Destruction of Jerusalem

Jeremiah and His Contemporary Prophets *(Southern Kingdom)*

Nahum 650 — 620

Zephaniah 636 — 623

Habakkuk 621 — 609

Jeremiah (53 years of ministry) 627 — 574

Ezekiel 593 — 559

Daniel 605 — 536

710 700 690 680 670 660 650 640 630 620 610 600 590 580 570 560 550 540 530

JERUSALEM IN THE TIME OF JEREMIAH

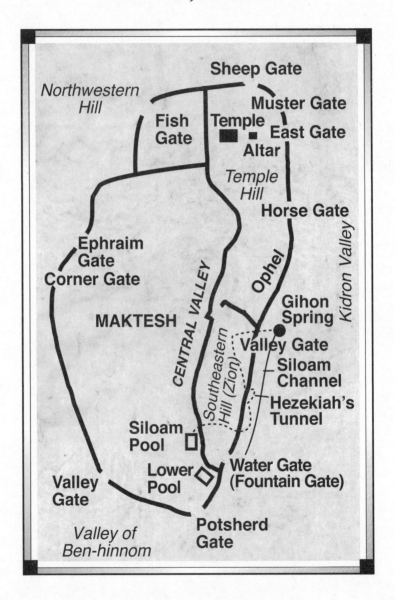

THE NATIONS OF JEREMIAH'S PROPHECY

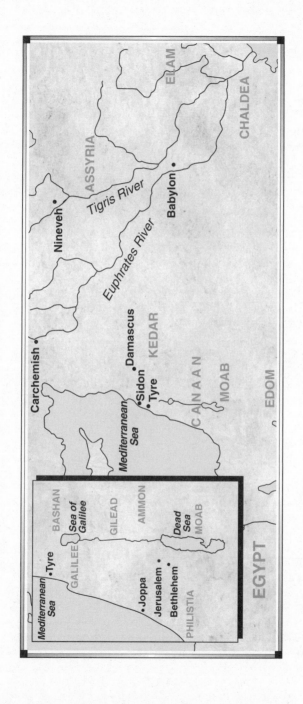

NOTES

1. KJV: whore; NIV: prostitute; ESV: whore
2. KJV, NKJV: affliction; NIV: disaster; ESV: trouble
3. KJV: spoil; NIV: ravage; ESV: devastate
4. KJV: full end; NIV: end; ESV: full end
5. KJV: hearken; ESV: pay attention
6. KJV: in vain; NKJV: false, falsehood; NIV: falsely; ESV:
7. KJV, NKJV, ESV: heritage
8. KJV, NKJV, ESV: pluck
9. NKJV, NIV: establish
10. NIV: plague
11. KJV: evil; NKJV, NIV: disaster; ESV: evil
12. KJV: turn away your captivity; NKJV: bring you back from your captivity; NIV: bring you back from captivity
13. KJV, NKJV, NIV: trouble
14. ESV: faithfulness
15. KJV: broken up; NIV, ESV: withdrawn
16. NIV: Lord Almighty

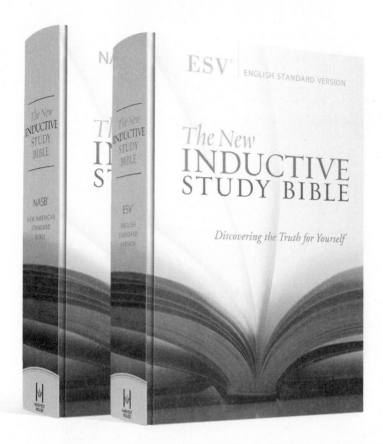

Books in the
New Inductive Study Series

❧ ❧ ❧ ❧

Teach Me Your Ways
Genesis, Exodus,
Leviticus, Numbers, Deuteronomy

*Choosing Victory,
Overcoming Defeat*
Joshua, Judges, Ruth

Desiring God's Own Heart
1 & 2 Samuel, 1 Chronicles

Walking Faithfully with God
1 & 2 Kings, 2 Chronicles

*Overcoming Fear
and Discouragement*
Ezra, Nehemiah, Esther

*Trusting God
in Times of Adversity*
Job

*Praising God Through
Prayer and Worship*
Psalms

*God's Answers for
Today's Problems*
Proverbs

*Walking with God
in Every Season*
Ecclesiastes, Song of Solomon,
Lamentations

Face-to-Face with a Holy God
Isaiah

Listening to God in Difficult Times
Jeremiah

What Is Yet to Come
Ezekiel

*God's Blueprint
for Bible Prophecy*
Daniel

*Discovering the God
of Second Chances*
Jonah, Joel, Amos, Obadiah

*Finding Hope
When Life Seems Dark*
Hosea, Micah, Nahum,
Habakkuk, Zephaniah

*Opening the Windows
of Blessing*
Haggai, Zechariah, Malachi

The Coming of God's Kingdom
Matthew

Experiencing the Miracles of Jesus
Mark

The Call to Follow Jesus
Luke

*The God Who Cares
and Knows You*
John

*The Holy Spirit
Unleashed in You*
Acts

*Experiencing the
Life-Changing Power of Faith*
Romans

*God's Answers for
Relationships and Passions*
1 & 2 Corinthians

*Free from Bondage
God's Way*
Galatians, Ephesians

That I May Know Him
Philippians, Colossians

*Standing Firm in
These Last Days*
1 & 2 Thessalonians

*Walking in Power,
Love, and Discipline*
1 & 2 Timothy, Titus

The Key to Living by Faith
Hebrews

*Living with Discernment
in the End Times*
1 & 2 Peter, Jude

God's Love Alive in You
1, 2, & 3 John,
Philemon, James

Behold, Jesus Is Coming!
Revelation